THE GOVERNORS OF TENNESSEE

THE PELICAN GOVERNORS SERIES

THE GOVERNORS OF TENNESSEE

Second Edition

Margaret I. Phillips

PELICAN PUBLISHING COMPANY
Gretna 2001

*The word "Pelican" and the depiction of a pelican are
trademarks of Pelican Publishing Company, Inc., and
are registered in the U.S. Patent and Trademark Office.*

Library of Congress Cataloging-in-Publication Data

Phillips, Margaret I.
   The governors of Tennessee / Margaret I. Phillips.—2nd ed.
     p. cm.
   "A Firebird Press book."
   Includes bibliographical references and index.
   ISBN 1-56554-826-4 (pbk. : alk. paper)
    1. Governors—Tennessee—Biography. I. Title.
F435.P48 2000
976.8'009'9—dc21
[B]

                              00-035960

Photographs are by the author unless otherwise noted.

Printed in the United States of America

Published by Pelican Publishing Company, Inc.
1000 Burmaster Street, Gretna, Louisiana 70053

*This book is for a special "first family"
in Tennessee, who somehow endured the
whole thing. . .*

Contents

Acknowledgments

Acknowledgment, together with my deepest appreciation is herewith offered to the following:

The librarians and archivists of the Tennessee State Library and Archives Department for supplying detailed information and the photographs for this publication; the librarian of the Nashville Public Library for her patience in extracting tedious, hard-to-find, current material; the Giles County and Lawrence County librarians for allowing me the continuous use of books until they were "way past due."

To Wilma Dykeman, noted Tennessee author, and William Rutherford, vice-president and historian in residence at Martin College, for reading and criticizing parts of the manuscript; to a fine group of students who read and verified historical dates and events "just one other time" for me; and to my typists, who struggled through stacks of my hurried longhand.

I am also indebted to three publications that have guided me in attempting a straight and detailed accounting of a complicated and diverse subject: to Dr. Stanley Folmsbee and his associates, Robert Corlew and Enoch

x ACKNOWLEDGMENTS

Mitchell, author of the scholarly text *Tennessee: A Short History*, and to Gentry R. McGee's simpler text, *History of Tennessee*, which has proved indispensable in helping me choose between the necessary facts and the superfluous jargon of the erudite. And finally, a special compliment is due Nancy Wooten Walker for her publication on Tennessee's first ladies, *Out of a Clear Blue Sky*, that has given me insight into the private lives of forty-six governors of Tennessee.

Preface

This is not a history, except in the events of the past that have touched the lives of men who shaped the state of Tennessee, those men who sat at its head and guided its course from the time of dirt roads that cut through the wilderness to lace together a province divided into three sections—East, Middle, and West Tennessee—and continuing to the era of glistening overpasses and junctions that skirt cities and towns and hold intact that same network, where men have learned to live peacefully together.

There has long been a need for a book such as this, where the lives of the state's leaders and its events can be brought together in some order, taken out of the vernacular of the lawmakers and placed in a chronological sequence to be read by the young and the old alike. It has not been possible to include an accounting of every event important to Tennessee, nor would the reader want it so; but if in the biographical sketches of *The Governors of Tennessee* I have shown something of the culture of the state in its developing stages, why then I have meant to.

To say that Tennessee first came into being on June 1, 1796, when the area was declared a state would be

to grossly err. Tennessee was here in 1492, somewhere
within the verdant wilderness that the courageous
Columbus glimpsed; it existed when De Soto first stood
and gazed into the dank delta along the Mississippi or
when the Frenchman named La Salle floated down that
same river from Quebec and built his fort Prudhomme near
the site of Memphis, one of other such forts built along
Tennessee rivers to hold the English beyond the Allegheny
Mountains where pushing in from Europe, they had
scattered along the valleys and settled by the hundreds
along the Atlantic coast. But neither fort nor mountain
could hold back the pioneer; he had crossed a greater evil
in his crude boat. At least here the earth gave him footing,
and this was his beginning in Tennessee.

Yet before any of these were the Indians, the docile
Shawnee first, roaming the land and living from its boun-
ties and later the more aggressive Cherokees and Creeks
and Chickasaws. And before these tribes there were the
mound builders, their identity and existence obscured by
the ripples of time. But they left their marks on the walls
of Tennessee's caves, their artifacts layered in limestone
crevices or buried beneath rounded mounds of fertile soil
over which powered farm machinery now quietly glides as
another generation works the soil, adding their part to the
state's perpetuity while helping to feed the nations'
millions.

So Tennessee began, but the formation of its government, with which this book is concerned, started much
later, in the spring of 1772, when a group of early settlers
gathered along the Watauga River, formed the Watauga
Association—which history records as the first American
attempt at self-government--the crux of which was the
struggle of free men to remain free. And from that
beginning, Tennessee has moved steadily forward, contri-
buting a glorious part to the development of the United

States, not only at state level, but at the national level as well. If there were an even distribution of presidents throughout the United States, there would be less than one president per state ratio; yet, Tennessee has contributed three, not to mention her copious share of cabinet officers.

J. W. Caldwell, in his *Sketches of the Bench and Bar*, describes that early school of Tennessee statesmen who filled those offices, especially the governor's chair: "Physically, they were lean and angular; mentally they were keen, aggressive, unrelenting in dislikes, faithful in friendships, and determined to a fault; morally they were not always above reproach in their private lives, but in public relations they were, almost without exception, sound to the core, and absolutely trustworthy. They were dangerous and often implacable enemies, the most faithful friends, and the sincerest patriots."[1] To Caldwell's thoughts I can only add my own for those early leaders who held the state's highest office, and for the later leaders as well—to have watched, to have projected, to have persuaded, and to have endeavored to leave the state a better place for their having sat at its head, that is to have governed.

Margaret I. Phillips

[1]Joshua W. Caldwell, *Sketches of the Bench and Bar* (Knoxville: Ogden Brothers and Company, 1898), 348.

THE
GOVERNORS
OF
TENNESSEE

1

The State of Franklin

JOHN SEVIER
(1784)

When the settlers came from Europe, pushing down the eastern seashore toward Virginia and the Carolinas, there was no dividing line between North Carolina and what was to become the state of Tennessee. North Carolina extended from the Atlantic Ocean to the Mississippi River, and today's Tennessee was then the western half of North Carolina, void of white settlers.

The Cherokee Indians occupied the mountains and valleys of the area now known as East Tennessee, while the Creek Indians lived along the Tennessee River in the southern part of Middle Tennessee. The Chickasaws inhabited the area on the high hills or bluffs along the Mississippi in West Tennessee where Memphis now stands, and the Chickamaugas lived around the region that is Chattanooga. All of the country bounded by the Cumberland Mountains, the Tennessee River, and the Ohio River was open; the tribes dared not take up residences in the area for fear of attacks by their peers over rights to the land. This open land, where wild animals were plentiful, became much sought-after by the pioneers traveling westward from Virginia and North Carolina, and they quickly established small settlements along its rivers.

These settlements were soon to be part of a new nation. America embarked upon the Revolutionary War with England and won its independence. While rejoicing in their newly found freedom, the former colonists discovered the transition to self-government was not easy. The new government was harassed by heavy indebtedness. To ease this burden of debt, Congress proposed that states which owned vacant lands throw them into common stock, cede them to the United States, and out of this joint fund the common debt could be liquidated.

North Carolina's open lands extending from the Alleghenies to the Mississippi River were becoming expensive and burdensome anyway, so in June of 1784, the state ceded them to the federal government. But the impression was that Congress would not formally accept the cession of the western territory for a period of two years. During that time, new settlements made by those first brave pioneers who had pushed on westward, thinking they were still in Virginia, settling along the Watauga River and the surrounding area, were to be neither under the protection of Congress nor of the parent state, leaving them without support from the United States or from England. There was no military organization to protect them, and violations of laws went unpunished. The country became infested with culprits fleeing punishment elsewhere, for here was a sort of seclusion for them. Indian aggression likewise grew rampant, and there was no authority to whom the settlers could turn for help.

Ceded from their parent state and not yet accepted by their federal owners, the inhabitants of the territory looked now to formation of an independent state so that laws could be maintained. They accused North Carolina of having been no more than a stepmother to them in the first place, and determined to organize themselves into a complete government. This they attempted and named

John Sevier
1784, 1796-1801, 1803-1809

John Sevier as their governor. At first they called the area Frankland and then Franklin, in honor of Benjamin Franklin.

When the governor of North Carolina learned of the activities beyond the mountains, he ordered the people to disband their newly formed government and return their allegiance at once to the state of North Carolina. The state legislature repealed the act of cession to the United States.

By now, many of the settlers had split into two factions over the issue. Some were despondent at trying to establish so sizable a thing as a government and were ready to return to the jurisdiction of North Carolina. Others were not, and the division in thought resulted in two political parties: the Franklin party with Sevier at the head, and the North Carolina party following John Tipton. Each party refused to honor the other as authoritative, and the result was chaotic. Public papers—marriage licenses, mortgages, deeds—recorded by one party were not recognized by the other. The Franklin party grew weaker and weaker, and when Sevier's term as governor expired in 1788, the state of Franklin was dead; thus the land and the people were again under the rule of North Carolina.

Sevier was arrested by Tipton—who held office under the state of North Carolina—and hauled back across the mountains to stand trial for attempting to form a separate state and for refusing to obey the governor who had ordered him to return to pay allegiance to North Carolina. At his trial, in a drama to equal any twentieth-century Western movie, his friends whisked him away from jail on horseback before the hearing started. Apparently neither the judge nor the jury was greatly upset over his escape, for Sevier was never tried and was soon thereafter restored by an act of the legislature to his former privileges. In 1789, he was elected a member of the United States Congress for the western district of North Carolina, making him the first congressman from the Mississippi Valley.

2

The Territory South
of the River Ohio

After the abortive state of Franklin failed, the territory
beyond the Alleghenies was again under North Carolina
rule. The latter, in order to provide for its representation,
apportioned itself into four districts. The western section
included all North Carolina territory "beyond the mountains," and this area was thus labeled the "Territory of the
United States of America South of the River Ohio."
William Blount was appointed by President Washington as
its governor; David Campbell was named judge of the
superior court, and John Sevier was made brigadier general
of Washington District (East Tennessee). James Robertson,
recorded in history as the father of the state of Tennessee
because of his courageous pioneer leadership, became
brigadier general of Miro District[1] (Middle Tennessee).
West Tennessee was not yet developed.

[1] So named by the North Carolina legislature at Robertson's request in
honor of Don Estevan Miro, Spanish governor of Louisiana. (Spelling later
evolved into "Mero.")

7

WILLIAM BLOUNT

(Democrat)
(1790-1796)

Now the stepchild of North Carolina west of the mountains had again been ceded to the United States government, and William Blount found himself its governor and superintendent of Indian affairs. Leaving his family behind temporarily, Blount traveled by horse into the territory to establish first himself and then a new government in the sparsely settled area. Dignified, well-mannered, and well-dressed, he sat tall in the saddle as he ambled through the area, studying the people and their problems. Though regarded as somewhat snobbish by the pioneers, Blount entertained a keen interest in them as individuals and especially in the western territory which they occupied. It was a time when land could be bought for a song if one had the price of the tune, and Blount did; so he kept his eye on the new country.

If the people thought their new governor a trifle smug, he may have had a right to be, if wealth and class status give one that prerogative. His ancestors were instrumental in establishing the Virginia Colony and had remained influential people among the landed gentry in the Virginia and North Carolina area. Thomas Blount, William's grandfather, was the third son of Sir Walter Blount of Worchestershire, England, who came to America in 1664 and settled in the Isle of Wight County, Virginia. Thomas, not only a wealthy landowner and planter and one of the country's first shipbuilders, had several other business enterprises as well, including lumber mills and metal works.

William Blount was born to Jacob and Mary Gray Blount in North Carolina on March 26, 1749. Jacob was wealthy in his own right, and William followed in like fashion. The future governor received his early education in his Episcopalian home; his formal training began at age fifteen, when a schoolteacher took up residence in Craven County where the family lived.

On February 12, 1778, Blount married Mary Grainger, a young woman of his own status. Early in their marriage he turned to a military and political career in an effort to help halt the British dominance that was running rampant in the colony. But all his energy was not expended in civil strife; he found the time to go into business with a brother, John Gray Blount, in a land developing enterprise. William did not relinquish this partnership when he accepted the position as governor to the new territory, and the Blount brothers' firm bought up over a million acres of the western land.

As governor, Blount appointed his half-brother, Willie Blount, one of his three secretaries, and set about at once to organize and establish counties in the area: first Washington, then Sullivan, Green, Hawkins, Davidson, Sumner, Tennessee, Knox, and Jefferson. He next saw that military organizations and courts were established in each county. It was an era when men slept with guns beneath their pillows, fearful for their scalps, and a military organization was the first matter of business in each county.

Blount selected Rocky Mount in the forks of the Holston and Watauga rivers as the first capital of the territory south of the Ohio, but later removed the seat of government to White's Fort which he renamed Knoxville, in honor of Henry Knox, the U.S. secretary of war who had greatly aided the pioneer families. The governor built a fine mansion in Knoxville, which was the first two-story house of sawed lumber west of the Allegheny Mountains.

Visitors were awed by the mansion's elegance, and the Indians called it the "snow house with glass eyes."[2]

Possibly, William Blount initiated a lifestyle that was to remain an eminent part of the lives of succeeding governors. He was a handsome, personable individual, and made it a part of his business to keep in contact with the dignitaries of his day, including President Washington at Mount Vernon. He and the territory's first lady, whom he had nicknamed Mosley, enjoyed attending dances and social events wherever possible, and they entertained often in their new mansion.

Mrs. Blount was a gracious and hospitable hostess in her elaborately furnished home. Political leaders were entertained in the ballroom or the formal dining room, while more ordinary individuals were just as welcome at the kitchen table. The Blounts' homelife, though often upset by illnesses, is recorded as that of a closely knit family group.

However, Blount could not maintain that atmosphere of dignified tranquillity in the territory. Hostile Indians, knowing the people were without the protection of North Carolina, made frequent attacks on the forts. The new American government urged patience in working out peaceful treaties with the Indians, but those settlers whose homes had been destroyed in these raids could not long abide a patient attitude and demanded retaliation. Too, the settlers were being taxed by the government for a protection that they were not receiving, and they held Blount responsible.

Blount had not received the following that he desired, nor had he brought a way of Eastern social structure and unity to the "West" as he had hoped to do. Hence, when

[2]Nancy Wooten Walker, *Out of a Clear Blue Sky: Lives of Tennessee First Ladies* (Knoxville: Nancy Walker, 1971), 26.

the territory was accepted into the Union in 1796 and became the state of Tennessee, the people failed to elect him again as governor, choosing instead John Sevier, who had proved himself a proficient leader of men already. Blount did, however, win a seat in the United States Senate.

Not only was the ex-governor plagued by the ascendancy of Sevier's popularity, but his land developing firm was now bankrupt. In truth, Blount could be described as a product of his culture—living in a day when land could be bought for a few cents an acre, he found the prospects of purchasing lands and selling them for a lucrative profit too tempting a business venture to ignore. Like others of his century who had shared accessible opportunities, Blount was charged with conspiracy as a land speculator. He was faced with impeachment and ousted from the Senate.

Returning to the state where he had first been governor, he sought and found refuge. Despite his bankrupt condition, Blount held his social prestige and—in Tennessee—his political image, albeit a trifle tarnished.

An epidemic of fever struck Knoxville around the turn of the nineteenth century, and the Blount household with its seven children was not excluded. Blount developed chills and fever, and died on March 21, 1800, having lived barely a half-century. His widow died two years later. Both were buried in Knoxville.

Blount College (now the University of Tennessee), established in 1794 by the territorial legislature, was named in his honor. The Blounts' daughter, Barbara Gray Blount, studied there as one of the first co-eds in America.

3

The State of Tennessee

By 1795 there were enough people in the territory—better than 60,000—to make the area a state. A convention was called at Knoxville in January, 1796, and that convention framed the first constitution of the state of Tennessee. Andrew Jackson officially proposed the name of the state, though it had been called the Tennessee Country for years, so named for the Tennessee River, derived from the Indian "Tenase." In June, 1796, President Washington signed the act which made Tennessee the sixteenth state of the American Union.

JOHN SEVIER
(Democrat)
(1796-1801; 1803-1809)

The government of Tennessee began to function when the legislature was organized on March 28, 1796; and on March 30, John Sevier was inaugurated governor of the new state. His record as a pioneer fighter possibly transcends his contribution as governor. In the records of the modern anti-discriminatory culture, when there is glimpsed a hint if not a definite admission that the Indians may have been treated unfairly by the white men, the accomplishments of

12

pioneer leaders such as Sevier could be questionable. Yet if judgment is to be passed, then it should be assessed according to the era in history in which the individual in question lived; and in Sevier's case, the society of which he formed a part was fraught with the task of survival. Not only was the pioneer's existence threatened by "savages," but by the extinction of the essentials for his life that could come only from the soil. Thus, as governor, Sevier encouraged the growth of the state's populace, wielding the influx of immigrants as a tool, pushing the Indians farther back. He vindicated his theory of expansion with his philosophy that the development of agriculture should be the main objective of the landowner, that no people were entitled to more land than they could cultivate, and that uncivilized Indians should be conceded no right to control vast acres of untilled land.

Sevier was born in Rockingham County, Virginia, on September 23, 1745. Of Huguenot ancestry, his fore-fathers first bore the name Xavier. When that religious sect fled France in the seventeenth century because of religious persecutions, Sevier's paternal grandfather was among them; he renounced his allegiance to France and emigrated to England, where he took the name of Sevier, and an English bride. Two of their children ran away from home and came to America. One of them, Valentine Sevier, settled in the Shenadoah Valley of Virginia and married Joanna Goade. John Sevier was the oldest of their seven children.

Though Sevier's level of education is unknown, he attended Augusta Academy, the forerunner of Washington and Lee University, and was believed to be one of the better educated men of his day. He married Sara Hawkins of a respectable Virginia family, and by age nineteen he had purchased land and had become a merchant in New Market.

Quite well-off as a merchant, Sevier was attracted to stories told of life beyond the Alleghenies. He visited a brother who had already settled in the area and remained there for a time himself. In 1773, he moved his wife and children and his parents into the new settlement on Holston River, but shortly thereafter they pushed on to the Watauga settlement.

Sevier's potential for leadership was at once evident to the settlers; his perseverance and natural dignity marked him for the militia, in which he promptly received distinction for both his strategy and his stamina as he led the volunteer soldiers in protection of their forts against the vicious attacks of the Cherokees. History records him as having led thirty-five successful fights against the Indians as well as the historical battle against the British at King's Mountain, and his celebrated war cry "Here they are! Come on, boys" has become legendary to Tennesseans.

Sevier held the confidence and respect of the pioneers. Therefore when the territory in which the settlers found themselves estranged was released by North Carolina and they attempted to organize their own governing body, they at once elected John Sevier their governor. Though the "state of Franklin" was doomed to failure and Sevier was charged with high treason, being accused of levying troops to oppose North Carolina's government and of killing good citizens with an armed force, and though charged further with underhanded land speculations in much the same manner as Blount before him, Sevier's followers refused to acknowledge his actions as anything less than heroic.

He served as Tennessee's high executive for twelve years, encountering the problems of establishing a government in a rapidly growing frontier territory whose two major cities—Nashboro (Nashville) on the Cumberland River and Knoxville in East Tennessee were divided by

200 miles of Indian-held wilderness. But Sevier's talent for peaceful negotiations in securing tribal lands proved as effective as his fighting prowess when he headed the militia. He established numerous treaties with the Indians during those twelve years, laid constructive plans for legislation, opened new wagon roads into the state, and encouraged the entrance of new settlers.

Robertson County (named for James Robertson) and Montgomery County (for Colonel John Montgomery) were created by Sevier from the original Tennessee County originally established by Blount. That county was absolved when the state took Tennessee as its title.

Sevier was the acknowledged political and personal enemy of Andrew Jackson, and pages of history are flecked with verbal abuses hurled between the two. Despite the eighteenth-century Jackson charisma, Sevier had a strong following. He served three consecutive terms as governor from 1796 to 1801, and when he could not succeed himself after his third term, the people elected Archibald Roane to replace him. But at the close of Roane's first term in office, the voters promptly elected Sevier again, and he served another three successive terms.

At the close of his sixth term as governor, John Sevier was elected to the state senate for one term, and then to the Congress where he remained until his death. He died of fever on September 24, 1815, while on a congressional mission for Fort Decatur, Alabama (Creek Indian Country), and was buried on the east bank of the Tallapoosa River. Ironically enough, his grave remained practically unrecognized for years in the wilderness of the pioneer country that he so fervently tried to develop; but in 1887 his dust, or whatever remained of him after seventy-two years, was removed to Knoxville where a marker bares his contributions and his famous war cry "Come on, boys. Come on!"

"Chucky Jack" (nickname derived from his Noli-chucky River farm) was the father of eighteen children, ten by his first wife—who died during an Indian uprising and was buried at night in the wilderness, her grave covered over by brush to prevent its desecration by the Indians—and eight by a second wife, Catherine Sherrill Sevier, who earned her own place in Tennessee history by jumping a stockade into Sevier's arms while fleeing Indian pursurers. The charming Sevier termed his catch "Bonnie Kate," and she became the stepmother to his ten children and the first of Tennessee's first ladies.

ARCHIBALD ROANE
(Democrat)
(1801-1803)

In contrast to the charismatic John Sevier, Archibald Roane was a cultivated, scholarly individual. He was fond of literature, well-versed in the classics, courteous of manner, and was an educator at heart. Born in what is now Dauphin County, Pennsylvania, in 1760, Archibald was the oldest child of Andrew and Margaret Roane, who emigrated from Ireland in 1739. (When the Roanes moved there, that part of Pennsylvania was known as Donegal and Derry, later called Lancaster.) Andrew Roane, a weaver, died at an early age and left his four children to the care of his brother John.

Archibald displayed a fine intellect, and was left a legacy of twenty pounds by his uncle to be applied toward a college education, which he put to good use. After studying at Lancaster for a while, he left college to join the Continental army with which he fought until the close of the Revolutionary War. He crossed the Delaware with

William Blount
1790-1796

Willie Blount
1809-1815

Archibald Roane
1801-1803

Joseph McMinn
1815-1821

General Washington on Christmas Eve in 1776, and was on hand at the surrender of Yorktown.

At the close of the war, Roane became a teacher at Liberty Hall Academy in Rockbridge, Virginia, and later studied law. He then moved to Tennessee and, as a young lawyer, was appointed district-attorney general and was a member of the convention that helped frame the state constitution in 1796.

John Sevier had to step down from the gubernatorial chair in 1801, following six years of leadership, and Roane was elected to succeed him. The state grew and prospered under his direction, and was divided into three congressional districts--Washington, Hamilton, and Mero. Jackson County was organized, and the state seal was designed. The latter was produced by William and Matthew Atkinson of Knoxville, who were paid one hundred dollars for manufacturing both the seal and the press to use it. Governor Roane first applied it on April 24, 1802.

Andrew Jackson had come into the new state about the same time as the governor. Soon after Roane took office, the major-general of the militia died, and the candidates for his replacement were Jackson and his bitter enemy, John Sevier. Although Sevier was some twenty years older than Jackson and more experienced in battle, the vote was seventeen to seventeen between the two men. Roane had to cast the deciding vote which went to Jackson, starting the latter on the military career that finally led to the presidency of the United States.

While Roane's intellectual qualifications earned him the respect he merited, they were not essential qualifications for a leader of the pioneer period. The settlers needed men of action, men who revealed a fighting prowess and would protect their property and families, not scholarly thinkers. Perhaps partly for this reason, Roane lost his second bid for the governorship to the people's hero, John Sevier, who again ran for governor in 1803. The people were still Sevier's friends and voted almost unanimously for him the second time. He remained in office until 1809.

Though well-educated for his day, Roane wrote few papers. Composition was apparently distasteful to him. He had a high sense of justice and integrity, but is said to have lacked the insight and forcefulness requisite for leaving a deep and lasting impression on the populace and the legal system of his day.

The major interest in his life seems to have been teaching, the profession to which he returned for a while after he left the governor's chair. At one time he was the instructor of Hugh Lawson White, who became a candidate for president of the United States in 1836. Roane also served as trustee of Greeneville College, Blount College (now the University of Tennessee), and of Washington College in Washington County, the first three incorporated colleges in the state.

He was appointed one of the superior court judges of law and equity in 1811, his last official office. At his retirement he returned to his "Grassy Valley" estate in Knox County.

In 1788 he had married Ann Campbell, of Campbell's Station in Knox County, and the couple had nine children. His wife was the daughter of Mary Hamilton Campbell and David Campbell of Abingdon, Virginia.

Roane, an Episcopalian, died at age sixty in this home on January 18, 1819, preceding his widow by twelve years. His grave in Pleasant Forest Cemetery near Campbell's Station was unmarked for almost a hundred years until the state erected a monument to his memory in June, 1918. Roane County was named in his honor.

Sevier took over the governorship for another six years. When his last term ended, Tennessee had over 260,000 people, including Indians. Indian boundaries had been established, religious movements had started in the state and denominations were spreading, and inhabitants had moved from East Tennessee on into Middle Tennessee.

WILLIE BLOUNT
(Democrat)
(1809-1815)

Willie (pronounced Wylie) Blount, who followed John Sevier's sixth term, was born in Bertie County, North Carolina, on April 17, 1768. He was the oldest son of Jacob Blount and his second wife, Hannah Salter Baker Blount. A half-brother to William Blount, Tennessee's territorial governor, Willie studied at Princeton and Columbia, and read law with a North Carolina judge. In 1790 he moved to the territory of Tennessee where he served as one of William's three private secretaries following the latter's gubernatorial appointment.

He was licensed to practice law in 1794, and in 1796 the first legislature of Tennessee elected him as one of the judges in the newly constituted state, but he resigned the office. The following year, the voters of Montgomery County chose him for the state legislature where he served one term.

In 1802, Willie married Lucinda Baker, daughter of Major John and Ann Norfleet Baker, also of Bertie County. The couple had two daughters of their own and were also responsible for rearing the younger children of William and Mary Blount following their early deaths only two years apart.

Blount sought the company of leaders and the elite, men such as Andrew Jackson, John Sevier, and Archibald Roane. He won the election for governor in 1809, defeating

William Cooke, one of the most influential men of the state, by about 3,000 votes; he was reelected in 1811 and in 1813.

Congenial and respected by his contemporaries, though lacking the brilliance of his brother William and of Sevier, Willie Blount served the state well, encouraging a policy of public improvements that included better methods of travel and transportation by opening new roads to the pioneering families as they looked for open markets and new occupations in a growing state.

By 1814 the state's population numbered some 300,000, and the Bank of the State of Tennessee had been established in Knoxville with branches erected at Clarksville, Columbia, Jonesboro, and Nashville. There were problems to be handled, too, not the least of which was agitation of the Indians by anti-Americans.

During Blount's administration the physical geography of the state was slightly changed. In 1811 earthquakes were felt in the area near the Mississippi River from the mouth of the Ohio to Vicksburg. In West Tennessee the shocks were severe, leaving great cracks in the earth. The mouth of Reelfoot River was lifted up, and for miles along its course the land sank far below the country around it. The sunken places were afterward filled with water, forming the famous Reelfoot Lake from which Lake County takes its name.

Blount is best remembered for the aid he gave to General Jackson during the Creek War and the War of 1812 when, in response to Jackson's request for money and men with which to fight, Blount raised $370,000 plus 2,000 volunteer soldiers within Tennessee. The act contributed to Jackson's successful victory in the historical Battle of New Orleans in 1815, and Tennessee received its "Volunteer State" epithet as the result of the patriotic enthusiasm displayed in the state; Governor Blount was likewise cited by President Madison for his patriotic zeal as the state's leader.

When his three terms expired, Willie Blount left the governor's chair to Joseph McMinn, and returned to his plantation home in Montgomery County, where he lived the life of a prosperous planter. He enjoyed writing, expounding his thought in religious discourses. He began a history which he called "The Constitution of the United States and Tennessee," but the work was never finished.

In 1827 he again sought the governorship but was defeated by Sam Houston. Representation of Montgomery County at the Constitutional Convention of 1834 was apparently his last involvement in political affairs.

His wife having preceded him in death by five years, Blount died at his home on September 10, 1835. He was buried in a private burial ground near Port Royal. His remains were moved to Greenwood Cemetery in Clarksville in 1877 and a monument was erected in his honor by the legislature.

J O S E P H   M c M I N N
(Democrat)
(1815-1821)

Joseph McMinn was a strong-willed, rustic frontiersman whose controversial private life set its own precedent, yet he never lost his following. He was congenial and honest and possessed his share of common sense, and these were the major requisites for leadership in his day.

Fifth of ten children, he was born in Chester County, Pennsylvania, on June 27, 1758, to Robert and Sarah Harlan McMinn, both Quakers. Although his degree of education is somewhat uncertain, it was of such as his area offered. As a member of the Friends' Church, he was taught not to believe in war and violence, but the church allowed each member to decide for himself whether to engage in warfare, and it is recorded in *Notable Men of Tennessee,* that he was involved in the Revolutionary War.[1]

Soon after the close of the war, McMinn left Philadelphia, venturing across the mountains into the new land of Tennessee. He settled in Sullivan County, which later became Hawkins County. Here he married Hannah Cooper who had come into Tennessee with her parents from Virginia. He bought a farm in the area and for a time settled into the typical pioneer life, with Hannah working beside him in their fields. They had one daughter, Jane.

Revealing his first political interest in the militia, McMinn served as sergeant and then commander general. He also became a merchant which, if one were not a lawyer, seemed to be a boost toward the bottom rung of the political ladder in the early nineteenth century. William Blount, territorial governor, gave McMinn his first political appointment, naming him to a county office. He was a member of the territorial legislature of 1794, and in 1796 he helped frame the first constitution of Tennessee. His neighbors sent him to the state senate in 1807 where he served as speaker until 1809.

Hannah McMinn died in 1811, and the following year Joseph married Rebecca Kinkead. She bore him no children and died on January 11, 1815, about two weeks before his daughter, Jane McMinn Gains, died. Neither did Jane leave any offspring.

In the same year that he lost his second wife and his daughter, McMinn entered the race for governor. He ran against four influential men: Jesse Wharton, who had resigned from the United States Senate to become a candi-

1John Allison (ed.), *Notable Men of Tennessee* (Atlanta: Southern Historical Association, 1905), I.

date; Thomas Johnson, who had served in the legislatures of both North Carolina and Tennessee; Robert C. Foster, an ex-speaker of the house in the state legislature; and Robert Weakley, a former member of Congress and a delegate to the convention to ratify the constitution of the United States. All four of his opponents sent out circulars implying that they had become candidates at the request of their fellow citizens while McMinn merely made it clear that he was running upon his own announcement because he wanted to be governor. He won the election.

The following year he married a third wife, Nancy Glasgow Williams, who was the mother of four sons by a previous marriage. Her father, James Glasgow, had been secretary of the state of North Carolina in 1777-78. The third marriage was unsuccessful. Nancy accused her husband of getting on his horse and riding away, leaving her alone for weeks at a time while he lived with Indian tribes.

But however stormy his marriage, McMinn's administration did not suffer. On the contrary, it was noted for its fairness. The rights of the minority were respected, and in his amicable relations with the Indians McMinn was able to successfully negotiate for numerous acres of land, expanding the white settlements—an attribute not to be overlooked by early settlers; the most important occurrence of McMinn's administration, in fact, was the settlement of West Tennessee. Unlike East and Middle Tennessee, where the clash of tomahawks and rifles had advanced expansion, West Tennessee's fertile lands were peacefully taken from the Indians through quiet negotiations. And the Chickasaws, encouraged to hunt over the area after the first white settlements were made along the rivers, pushed back the bears and the panthers, making easy the pioneers' entrance. The country developed rapidly in this part of Tennessee, more so than in any other section, for with no threat of war hanging over them the people could give their attention to building roads and bridging streams.

The counties of Obion, Weakley, Henry, Byer, Gibson, Carrol, Tipton, Haywood, Madison, Henderson, Shelby, Fayette, Hardeman, McNairy, and Hardin all developed under McMinn's six years in office, and the state capital was changed from Knoxville to Murfreesboro. Governor McMinn was reelected in 1817, defeating Robert C. Foster, and again in 1819, winning over Enoch Parsons.

His homelife, meanwhile, was still troublesome, and his wife left him. Divorce, almost a new term in that new land, was not easily acquired. But McMinn brought a petition before the Tennessee House of Representatives requesting his freedom. Nancy, on the other hand, had the loquacious Felix Grundy of Nashville plead her rebuttal. When the deciding votes were counted, there were nineteen in favor of divorce and twenty in opposition. The couple agreed to a separation and lived apart until their deaths. Mrs. McMinn chose a fashionable environment in Nashville where she died at eighty-six. McMinn retired to a farm which he bought near Calhoun on the Hiwassee River about ten miles from Cleveland.

He spent the last two years of his life—from 1822 to 1824—as an agent for the Cherokee Indians and died at the Indian Agency on November 17, 1824. He was buried near Calhoun in McMinn County, leaving no descendants.

McMinn County and the town of McMinnville in Warren County are named in his honor.

WILLIAM CARROLL
(Democrat)
(1821-1827; 1829-1835)

If Sevier was Tennessee's cavalier fighter, Roane its scholar, Willie Blount the patriotic zealot and McMinn the peaceful negotiator, then William Carroll was surely the pioneering Babbitt. The new state was filling up with immigrants, and Carroll looked to its development from the businessman's point of view. Rivers had to be cleared of logs for better navigation, streams had to be bridged, and a wilderness crossed with roads that would join East, Middle, and West Tennessee. Business enterprises must be established that would provide jobs for the people.

Carroll left a deep imprint on the history of the state, primarily because he met a specific need at a specific time. He was elected for the gubernatorial office in 1821, and served three successive terms. Sam Houston took the governor's chair the term following, after which Carroll was again elected and stayed another six consecutive years. Politician that he was, Carroll also allowed himself to be nominated for a fourth term, for under the new constitution that had been written the previous year, a fourth term in office was possible. But all the populace was not so politically briefed, and felt that a fourth term was in violation of the constitutional provision in force at the time. Too, Carroll was a staunch Jackson supporter, and Jackson, then president of the United States, was backing Carroll for a fourth term as governor; the people felt Jackson's influence was becoming too dominant in the state and wanted the tide turned.

Serving the state longer than any other governor besides John Sevier, Carroll offered advice to the people of Tennessee which is as timely today as when he assumed the governorship over 150 years ago: He urged the people to use their common sense, work harder, pay their debts, spend less and save a little, stop spending money on foreign goods, tend to their own business and to give up the idea of luck or Providence or a public officeholder tending to it for them.

A man of wit with a keen mind, Carroll was born near

Pittsburgh, Pennsylvania, on March 3, 1788. He was the son of Thomas Carroll and Mary Montgomery Carroll, the oldest of their nine children. When he was around eighteen years of age, he moved with his parents to Davidson County, Tennessee. Here his education was limited, but he mastered a small amount of grammar, bookkeeping, surveying, and mathematics, and early took a job with a merchant who revealed confidence in his abilities and encouraged his growth in business affairs.

At twenty-two Carroll borrowed money and ventured into business for himself, opening the state's first nail store in Nashville, which then had a population of approximately 1,100. The business was highly successful, but young Carroll had a yen for military life, and gave up his nail store to join the state militia of which Andrew Jackson was commander-in-chief. By 1812 he had become captain of the Nashville Uniform Volunteers, and soon after that General Jackson appointed him brigadier-inspector and then major of the militia.

Like Jackson, Major Carroll showed his hand at dueling, wounding Jesse Benton on one occasion, and getting into a tiff with Jackson over a second duel with Thomas Benton. But their differences were settled during the military endeavors of the Creek War and the Battle of New Orleans, where Carroll's prowess as a fighter became evident.

Following the War of 1812, Carroll became the owner of the first steamboat registered in Nashville, the *Andrew Jackson*. Built at Pittsburgh at an approximate cost of $16,000, the vessel was supposedly the first boat to enter the waters of the Cumberland, an event which marked the opening of the Mississippi River to American vessels.

At the time of Carroll's entry into politics, another "first" occurred; newspapers became involved in the campaign for governor. The *Whig*, a leading publication established by William Brownlow, who would also one day be governor, supported Carroll; and the *Clarion,* a Nashville paper, supported Carroll's opponent, Edward Ward. Carroll defeated Ward 31,290 to 7,294 votes.

Under Carroll's twelve-year administration, the state gradually came out from the pioneer stage. It increased in population and wealth, cultivation expanded, the log gave place to more comfortable homes, settlements widened, hamlets became towns and towns became cities. New counties were established, schools, churches, and courthouses were built; public improvements were planned—and hindered by the incompetence of government—and manufacturers and commerce started to flourish.

The state constitution of 1796 had been outgrown and the people demanded a new one, especially for the purpose of levying taxes and electing officials. In a wail that has since become universal, the little man complained that he wasn't being justly treated, that taxes were lighter in proportion on large landowners than on small ones; and under the old constitution, only the governor and members of the legislature were elected by the people. The new constitution was established in 1834, toward the end of Carroll's tenure, after a laborious 104 days of effort by lawmakers.

The 1796 constitution had placed equal valuation on all land, partly as a means of encouraging immigrants to enter the new state, and partly, since the land was undeveloped, because the value was unknown. The only exception was the town lot, which could be taxed as high as 200 acres of open land. The new constitution, drawn up in Nashville in 1834, would allow all property to be taxed according to its value, that value to be determined in such manner as the legislature directed.

The document's other major provision gave the voters the right to elect county officials, whereas under the old constitution, members of the country courts—chosen by the legislature for life—elected the sheriffs, trustees, coroners, and other such officials.

Carroll's first three successive terms ended in 1827, when Sam Houston became governor. Houston left office in mid-term and William Hall assumed the gubernatorial chair for a brief period. When Carroll again took office in 1829, he carried out some of the proposals set up by Governor Hall, including the completion of the first penitentiary in Tennessee. The prison, finished in 1831, was built one-half mile west of Nashville and cost a little less than $50,000. Carroll advocated closing the affairs of the Bank of Tennessee, using a part of the capital to build roads across the state. That bank was dissolved and the Union Bank of the State of Tennessee was chartered with a capital of $3 million. The state took $500,000 of the stock of this bank and issued 500 five-percent bonds of $1,000 each.

The insurrection of Negroes in Virginia worried lawmakers, who passed a statute in relation to slaves and free persons of color. Free persons of color were not permitted to enter Tennessee, and owners of slaves were forbidden to emancipate them unless the slaves were immediately removed from the state.

Carroll encouraged internal improvements within the state, soliciting funds for such projects. Numerous changes were made in government; brutal punishment for petty crimes and misdemeanors was abolished, supplanted by terms of hard labor; imprisonment for debt was ended; a chancery court was established; doctors started using quinine for treating fevers; and a public school system was attempted.

The noted philanthropist Dorothea Dix, pioneering the cause of the mentally handicapped, had aroused the country's concern, and an act was passed to erect the state's first asylum. The building was completed near Nashville in 1840, and so great was the need for it that it soon proved inadequate in size and a larger one had to be built shortly thereafter near Murfreesboro.

More changes took place in the state under Carroll than under any other governor. The state capital had been moved to Nashville from Murfreesboro in 1826, during his first term in office, but no capitol building—as he had hoped to see established—was built there until 1845.

At twenty-five, the governor had married Cecelia Bradford, daughter of Henry Bradford of Fauquier County, Virginia, and the former Elizabeth Payne Blackmore. Henry Bradford was a well-to-do planter and plantation owner.

William Carroll died on March 22, 1844, and was buried in the City Cemetery at Nashville. Carroll County bears his name.

SAM HOUSTON
(Democrat)
(1827-April, 1829)

Sam Houston had to be Tennessee's most colorful governor. Better than six feet in height and well proportioned, the thirty-six-year-old bachelor cut a graceful figure as he campaigned for the governorship on his dapple-gray. His bell-crowned hat, standing coat collar, ruffled shirt and black trousers, and silk socks lavishly embroidered above his patent-leather shoes set off with silver buckles were in bold contrast to the leather moccasins and Indian attire that marked him for the man that he was at heart.

Of Scotch-Irish descent, Houston was born in Rockingham County, Virginia, on March 2, 1793. His father, Sam Houston, Sr., an inspector in the Virginia militia and a distinguished soldier in the Revolutionary War, died in 1807, and left Elizabeth Paxton Houston to support their nine children.

Sam Houston
1827-1829

Hoping to make a better living for her children in the West—West being any area that lay beyond the Allegheny Mountains—Mrs. Houston moved her family to Blount County, the extreme frontier at that time. She settled near her relatives on land that had been previously purchased by her late husband, and sought to make a living for them from the soil.

Sam Houston was around fifteen years of age when he came with his mother to Tennessee, and only six months of those years had been spent in the classroom. But that was enough time for him to learn how to read and write, and after moving to Blount County he entered Maryville Academy for a few more months of study. There he encountered literature, which he loved, especially Pope's translation of the *Iliad*.

Sam did not respond to farm life, preferring to lie under a tree and read while his brothers did the farm work; hence his family saw to it that he took a job as a clerk in a country store. Young Houston didn't adjust well to this work either, and shortly thereafter, taking his beloved copy of the *Iliad*, he ran away to live with the Indians. He found his way to the tent of John Jolly, a Cherokee chief, where he lived for some time. Even then, Houston studied the Indians' problems and surveyed their position as a minority group. He hoped to enter some type of work where he could see that the Cherokees had a fair opportunity in government affairs.

Because he had piled up debts during his stay with the Indians at Jolly Island, near Dayton, Houston needed a way to earn enough money to clear his name. So he opened a school for young children, teaching the students himself, and charging eight dollars per year for each child. His venture was successful. He cleared his debt, and then moved on toward a position in military life, joining the Thirty-ninth United States Infantry. Soon a sergeant, and shortly thereafter commissioned an ensign, his regiment fought in the historical Battle of Horseshoe Bend where Houston was severely wounded. The wound prevented his accompanying his friend Andrew Jackson in the fight at New Orleans; but after the close of the war, he was stationed in New Orleans with the Thirty-ninth Regiment for a while.

After returning to Nashville, Houston was appointed Indian agent and negotiated treaties with the Cherokees. But upon conducting a delegation of Indians to Washington, he was met with charges of having violated the law in his efforts to prevent the smuggling of Negroes from the Spanish province of Florida into western states. The charge was refuted, but Houston was offended and resigned the position.

At twenty-five, and deeply in debt again, he entered the office of James Trimble in Nashville to study law. After six months of study (instead of the prescribed eighteen months), he passed the required bar examination and opened a law office in Lebanon. Shortly after embarking upon this career, he was made adjutant-general of Tennessee. By 1819 he had become district attorney of Davidson District with an office in Nashville, but he resigned this position after a year and went back into general practice.

In 1821 he was elected major-general of Tennessee, and in 1823 the people of the state sent him to Congress. He was reelected in 1825. Houston's popularity with Tennesseans, coupled with Jackson's backing, earned him the governor's chair by a majority of some 12,000 votes in 1827. Nashville was barely an infant city at the time of Houston's reign there, with an approximate population of some 6,000 persons, 1,000 of whom were slaves.

Possibly because Sam Houston belongs more to the state of Texas than to Tennessee, or perhaps because his personality overshadowed his contribution as governor, his achievements in the state's history are somewhat indistinct. However, his position among them earned him a place in the hearts of Tennesseans, where his name still remains near to a household word.

While governor of the state, Houston married Eliza Allen, the daughter of John and Letitia Saunders Allen of Gallatin. The Allens were influential people in Sumner County, and the elaborate wedding was an affair of great social signifiance. One of the wedding gifts included the silver service of Rachel Jackson, presented to the newlyweds by Andrew Jackson who was in mourning following his wife's death. He was not at the wedding, however, but was en route to Washington to become the president of the United States.

The marriage of Governor and Mrs. Houston was not successful. After only three months of life together, Eliza packed up her clothes and went home to her parents, and the governor laid down his reins of leadership without notice to the people and hied back to the Indians. William Hall was appointed to finish Houston's term in office, and that marked the latter's exodus from Tennessee's history.

Leaving Nashville, Houston once more sought solitude with an Indian tribe, again becoming active in Indian affairs. He was called Sam Son by the tribe's chief, and was referred to as The Raven by other Indians. And there, in what is now Oklahoma, he took a wife without civil ceremony from the Cherokee tribe. She was Tiana Rogers, daughter of Hedgeman and Jennie Rogers, and Houston called her the princess he had found amid the lights and shadows of the forest.

He built a huge log house for his bride where they lived in style, but he absolved his tribal marriage and left his accumulation—including his cattle, horses, and two slaves—to his Indian mate when he learned that Texas was at war. A free man again, Sam Houston headed for Texas to aid the republic in its fight for independence, etching for himself a still greater place in the nation's history. But that is another story, and one within itself.

Three years after wandering into Texas, Houston was named commander-in-chief of the Texas army, and led his forces to victory in the Texas Revolution. In 1859 he was elected governor of Texas. Meanwhile, the election of Abraham Lincoln as president of the United States forced a showdown on the question of secession. Houston refused to pledge allegiance to the Confederate government and was forced out of office.

Houston had gone to Texas in 1833 and in May of 1840 had married a third wife, Margaret Moffatt Lea of Marion, Alabama. She was the daughter of John (a Baptist minister) and Nancy Lea. This marriage was apparently Houston's most successful one. Margaret Houston gave him eight children and influenced him greatly, persuading him to give up drinking, swearing, and gambling—all his vices in fact except his tobacco-chewing—with which he refused to part. He also joined the Baptist Church.

Sam Houston died on July 26, 1863, at the family's plantation home in Huntsville, Texas. He was buried in Oakwood Cemetery near his home. Mrs. Houston moved her family to Independence, Texas, after her husband's death. She died there in 1867 during a yellow fever epidemic .

WILLIAM HALL
(Democrat)
(April 16, 1829-October 1, 1829)

Tennesseans hardly had time to consider the leadership abilities of William Hall in the five and one-half months that he served as governor following Houston's departure from the office, for they were still puzzling over the fact that so virile a man as Houston could have so vulnerable a spot as the heart. But when his wife left him after three months of marriage, Houston left the governor's chair; and Hall, who was speaker in the state senate, automatically became governor. By provision of the constitution, Hall remained in the office until that particular term was finished. He served from April until October, at which time the people again elected William Carroll (who had preceded Houston) for a second three terms.

Hall's brief period in office was too short a time to prove itself, and like the Houston administration, it leaves no marked or special features to the annals of the state. However, the Houston-Hall administration maintained the policies that Carroll before them had initiated. The considerations for improvement in the state included a revision of the penal code; establishment of a penitentiary; modification of punishments; strengthening the educational program, feeble as it was at the time; and attention was given to the unstable currency and usury of the period.

Governor Hall was born in Surry County, North Carolina, on February 1, 1775. His parents were Major William and Elizabeth Thankful Doak Hall. Selling their possessions in Mecklenburg, North Carolina, in 1779, the family started for Kentucky. But unable to get through the wilderness with his wife and children, Major Hall stopped at New River, Virginia, and bought land. They settled eventually along the Bledsoe Lick area (now known as Castalian Springs, near Gallatin).

During the Indian wars, the Hall family suffered the loss of seven members when they were ambushed by the red men, and Major Hall was scalped in the presence of young William who was twelve years old at the time. Two of the governor's brothers, two brothers-in-law, a sister and her child also lost their lives to the tomahawks.

William Hall once stated that he had suffered as much as anyone could have suffered in the settlement of the new country.

Having survived the massacre, Hall grew to manhood in the Castalian Springs community, and worked the land on which the family had settled. He became a prosperous planter and married Polly Alexander, who had come into Tennessee with her parents, William Locke and Mary Brandon Alexander of Iredell County, North Carolina. William Alexander had fought in the Revolutionary War, and six members of the Alexander family had signed the Mecklenburg Declaration of Independence in 1775.

Political life started for Hall when he was elected to the Tennessee House of Representatives in 1797. He had been sherriff of his county and a brigadier general in the Creek War. Like other early leaders, he was a friend and admirer of Andrew Jackson, and an approver of William Carroll's remarkable leadership as the state's governor. For six years, Hall served in the legislature, and was elected to the state senate in 1821. He remained in the senate until he became governor ad interim.

When he left the governor's seat, William Hall returned to his farm home, Locust Acres in Sumner County. In 1831 he was elected to Congress where he served one term, retiring in 1833 again to his home, where he enjoyed the fellowship of his eight children. He died there on October 7, 1856, and was buried in Sumner County.

NEWTON CANNON
(Whig)
(1835-1839)

Newton Cannon was the first Whig governor of Tennessee, and his administration was overshadowed from the start by political strife. William Carroll, running for a fourth term in his second administration, was the Democratic (or Jackson) candidate in opposition to Cannon, who was a National Republican (or White) candidate. Once again, national politics came in close touch with state government in Tennessee. Andrew Jackson was approaching the end of his second term as president of the United States, and he wanted to see Martin Van Buren his successor. But Hugh Lawson White, up to this time a friend of Jackson's, was also running for president.

Between the War of 1812 and Jackson's second term as president, his influence was paramount in Tennessee, and virtually so in the nation. He had picked up many friends as a result of his influence, and made many enemies. When he had become president, Jackson had appointed his friends to the available offices, and some Tennesseans did not approve, Cannon among them.

William Carroll, on the other hand, was a Jackson supporter. Likewise, Jackson wanted Carroll again for governor of Tennessee, and he made it plain to the populace. Cannon was supporting Hugh Lawson White for president. White, along with other Jackson supporters, was opposed to Van Buren as a presidential candidate. Next to Jackson, White was the most popular man in the state at the time. He had been one of the judges in the state supreme court and had followed Jackson as United States senator when Jackson resigned that position in 1825.

White was so popular with the people that a movement was begun to make him a candidate for the presidency. Such a step greatly displeased Jackson, and he at once sought to make a place for White in his cabinet, even suggesting that White become a candidate for vice-president on the ticket. When White declined all offers, Jackson heatedly threatened to make White's name odious. White

William Carroll
1821-1827
1829-1835

William Hall
1829

Newton Cannon
1835-1839

James Knox Polk
1839-1841

was not a man to take dictation, even from a friend, so he gave his consent to run for president.

Jackson came into the state in support of Van Buren, and likewise Carroll for governor, denouncing White as a Federalist and declaring that no one could be his friend and the friend of White at the same time.

In the estrangement between Jackson and White, many saw the opportunity they were looking for. They were tired of Jackson's dictation, so they elected Cannon governor. Opposition to Jackson formed the genesis of the Whig party in Tennessee, and the time when the White Whigs came into existence, although Hugh Lawson White never accepted the name for himself.[2]

Tennessee voted for White, but Van Buren was elected president (Andrew Jackson's influence was not locked within the mountains of Tennessee). The period from Van Buren's election to that of Lincoln in 1860 was the zenith of Tennessee's greatness. Due to the liberal laws passed by the new constitution, Tennessee progressed in population and wealth until, in a few years, it had become one of the richest and greatest states in the Union, and its political influence was felt in the nation. Thus more attention was given to national affairs than to the Cannon administration at the state level.

Newton Cannon was born in Guilford County, North Carolina, on May 22, 1781. His father, Minos Cannon, was born in Maryland but later moved into North Carolina, where he married Letitia Thompson. Newton was quite young when his parents migrated to Tennessee country, along with other pioneer families, as fifty men rode shotgun beside the caravan while the women and children peered anxiously from behind the wagons' canvases,

---

[2]Those opposed to Jackson were not called Whigs until 1834. Previously they were in the National Republican party.

fearing Indian attacks. Their first attempted move to Tennessee had been a futile effort, for they met Indians at Cumberland Gap and turned back. But on their second try, they got as far as the fort at Nashborough (Nashville); and the Cannons settled permanently in the area.

Educational opportunities were limited for young Newton, and he started out in life as a saddler, then became a merchant and a surveyor, and planned to stick with the trades. But politics intervened in that early exciting time in Tennessee, and his first step in that direction was to study law. Cannon became a lawyer and was elected a member of the legislature from Williamson County in 1811. From the legislature he went with the volunteers to the Creek War, where he served as colonel, and afterwards was elected to succeed Felix Grundy in the United States Congress.

Many years younger than Andrew Jackson, Cannon became his enemy and defied "Old Hickory"[3] whenever he could. Once, in a lawsuit, Cannon offended him; Jackson pointed a finger in the young lawyer's direction and warned, "Young man, I will mark you."[4] Such was the relationship between Jackson and Cannon when the latter took the governor's chair in 1835, where he remained for two terms.

Cannon's administration had no special influence on the affairs of the state, primarily for reasons already mentioned, and he was frowned upon by East Tennesseans as not forging through on internal improvements. The *Memphis Enquirer* in West Tennessee ridiculed his

[3]So named because of a battle in which Jackson had conquered the Indians' Old Hickory hunting ground, deemed by them as unconquerable by white men.

[4]Walker, *Out of a Clear Blue Sky,* 92.

position, labeling him a farm boy and a saddler. But Middle Tennesseans looked more favorable on the Cannon administration; for one thing, his period in office saw the end of an infamous land and river pirate gang, headed by John A. Murrel from Madison County. Murrel organized a band of thieves and ruffians that included notorious individuals all the way from Kentucky to New Orleans, and they terrorized members of the Southwest with their stealing and killing. He was finally caught in the act of stealing Negroes from a neighbor, and was imprisoned. Other members of his gang tried to take possession of Vicksburg, Mississippi, on the 4th of July, 1835, but they were captured and hanged by the citizens without trial.

Primarily, however, Cannon's four years in office were peaceful ones for the state. The vigorous administration of Carroll had paved the way; the constitutional convention of 1834 had made needed reforms in the state government, and with the passing of the pioneer era, the state could look to a period of growing wealth and culture. The Seminole War was fought in Florida in 1836, and according to custom, Tennesseans took their active parts in that.

In 1839 Cannon lost his bid for a third term in office, defeated by James K. Polk. He retired to his mansion on the Harpeth River near Franklin, where he died on September 16, 1841. He was buried in the family cemetery in Williamson County.

Cannon had two marriages. The first, in 1813, was to fifteen-year-old Leah Prior Perkins, daughter of William Perkins of Davidson County; she died two years after their marriage, leaving one son. Five years later Cannon took Rachel Starnes Welborn for a second wife; she was the daughter of General James Welborn of North Carolina. Eight children were born to the second union.

JAMES KNOX POLK
(Democrat)
(1839-1841)

James Knox Polk, who became the eleventh president of the United States, took over the governor's chair at an appropriate period for one who had started his ascension to the White House. At no time before had there been such political uproar in Tennessee—or in America for that matter—as in those months during Polk's administration, and his campaigns. It was a period of national excitement, politically speaking, and affairs of the state were left pretty much to run themselves. Each political party had turned its whole attention to the national presidential election of 1840 and the contest between William Henry Harrison and Martin Van Buren. And Polk, orator that he was, fit right into the scene.

James K. Polk was born in Mecklenburg County, North Carolina, on November 2, 1795. His father was Samuel Polk, whose family had originally spelled the name Pollok. The Polloks had come to Maryland in 1680 and gradually moved down to North Carolina; and Samuel, a descendant of that group of emigrants, had married Jane Knox, great-grandniece of the famous Scottish clergyman John Knox.

When he was approximately ten years of age, James Polk came to Tennessee with his family. A frail, unhealthy child, he found it hard to adapt to frontier life, and his weakness was a constant disappointment to his father who desired to teach his sons farming and land surveying, the vocational requisites of the frontiersman. By the time young James was fourteen, it became apparent that he was suffering from a serious ailment; so his father took him by horseback to visit a pioneering young surgeon, Dr. Ephraim McDowell, in Danville, Kentucky. Dr. McDowell diagnosed gallstones and performed surgery with only brandy as an anesthesia. From this ordeal, Polk gained a sense of inward strength and made up his mind to dispense with menial labors and study to enter a professional work.

Polk's mother, a devout Presbyterian and a member of a well-to-do family, insisted that if her son lacked the stamina for farming, then there were other things that he could do. She at once set him on a course of study with a Presbyterian minister, in the hope of making him a man of the cloth. But James Polk was more materially than spiritually inclined, and looked instead to a life in law. He studied at Murfreesboro College and then went to the University of North Carolina, where he was graduated with academic honors in 1818. (Polk was the first college graduate to take the governor's chair.)

Following Polk's graduation, his father bought a set of used law books for him and established him in a law office in Columbia, where he studied law with Felix Grundy. He soon became a leading lawyer in the Maury and Giles County areas. Polk showed the potential for a political career, and quickly gained distinction as a colorful public speaker. A determined follower of Andrew Jackson, he was dubbed "Young Hickory" by his peers.

On January 21, 1824, Polk married Sara Childress, daughter of Joel and Elizabeth Whitsett Childress, whose family had also come from North Carolina and settled in Sumner County. Joel Childress built the first house and was the first postmaster of Murfreesboro.

Sara Childress, an educated young woman for her day, encouraged Polk to seek public office, which he did. He first served in the state legislature, and in 1825 was elected to Congress where he remained an active political figure for seven congressional terms, serving as Speaker of the House from 1835 to 1839.

In the 1839 gubernatorial campaign, Governor Cannon

was running for his third term, and he canvassed the state in joint debate with Polk. Cannon's arguments were strong, but he was a slow and cautious speaker whereas Polk—Napoleon of the Stump—was clever and witty, regaling crowd with amusing anecdotes at Cannon's expense. However, there couldn't be too much strife between Cannon and Polk, for they had to share the same room and usually the same bed at night on their campaign trail across the state, where private homes and rooming houses were their overnight accommodations.

Evidently, Polk's debating tactics were effective, for he defeated the incumbent and won the governorship. He soon found, however, that his administration was overshadowed by the contest between Harrison and Van Buren. Andrew Jackson had stepped down from the presidency in 1837, and wanted Martin Van Buren, who had succeeded him, to remain in the White House for another term. The Democrats, who still favored Jackson, were just as determined as he that Van Buren remain; and the Whigs were just as determined that he would not. Newspapers got into the fight with all their humor and sarcasm--but invective has yet to spoil a campaign for Tennesseans, and it didn't hurt this one. There were conventions and barbecues and drums and firecrackers and enough rhetoric to stir the deepest doldrums of any who pressed to the gatherings to hear the "big speeches."

Although Polk was a man of considerable wealth and belonged to the "upper class," he placed himself on the side of the people's government, against those who believed that the property owners and businessmen were better for the people, than the common-majority rule. He looked unfavorably on the national banking system and the construction of more roads in the country, but advocated the sale of American free lands, applying the money to public education. Believing that unenlightened people could not long remain free, he wanted all persons to have the chance at education.

Polk was against a congressionally appointed president, and had proposed a bill while in Congress whereby the power to elect the highest official in the land would lie directly in the hands of the people. Conscientious in serving the people who had elected him to a place of service, he went out of his way to favor his supporters, and once making up his mind on an issue, he refused to be swayed by the opinion of others. His political ideals conflicted with former friends, Felix Grundy in particular. By the end of his term, Polk's followers had fallen away to the point that his second bid for the governorship was unsuccessful. He ran for the office again in 1843 and lost that race as well.

In 1844, however, at the Baltimore Democratic Convention, Polk was nominated for the presidency of the United States. He was elected as the country's first dark horse candidate, in that he had not been groomed for the race (the party had decided not to run Van Buren again at the last moment). The ex-governor emerged from the contest as the eleventh president of the United States, even though he failed to carry his own state in the election.

During his term as president, Polk directed the country's efforts in the Mexican War by which California and approximately 500,000 square miles of the Southwest were added to the United States. Many Northerners were not pleased with the annexation, for they feared it would extend slave territory.

Even though Polk was a slaveholder himself, he could not conscientiously support human bondage. Since he refused to use his high office to promote slavery, many of his friends, themselves slaveholders, wanted to see him out of the White House. His staunchness of opinion and undaunted effort to serve the Union well had caused controversy, and he did not seek a second term.

History has recorded Polk as one of the harder working American presidents. Tuesday and Friday evenings were set aside at the White House for callers—no appointments were necessary. He spent hours at his desk writing his decisions and opinions in a diary that would not gain recognition until almost a century later, when historians and biographers began to deem him a truly great president. So busy was Polk that he refused to take the time to go to the barber shop; he cut his own hair.

The first lady allowed no callers on Sunday mornings, however, but made it a point to hustle the president off to the Presbyterian church with her in time for services. Although Polk had adhered to the discipline of a religious life, he did not formally unite with any church until six days before his death. He had returned to his home in Nashville, where he lay dying from cholera. It was then that he called in a Methodist minister, and was baptized into his preferred denomination.

James K. Polk died on June 15, 1849. He was buried in the City Cemetery and later his remains were removed to the state capitol grounds where his childless widow, who succeeded him by more than forty years, was buried beside him in 1891.

JAMES CHAMBERLAIN JONES
(Whig)
(1841-1845)

The Whigs chose James Chamberlain Jones as their candidate for governor in 1841, pitting him against Polk who was seeking a second term. Polk had long since proved his powers of oratory in the state, but the loquacity of his opponent proved a hurdle for him, as the Whigs well knew it would. Jones was not the educated speaker Polk was, but eloquency was not the concern of the speech-mad public; their delight was in seeing Polk's embarrassment as Jones ridiculed him in amusing antics that brought roars of laughter.

Over six feet tall and weighing only 125 pounds, "Lean Jimmy" Jones was apparently the cut-up of the century. He was a natural mimic and actor, and made jokes of Polk's arguments in debate. Polk lost his temper while Jones—with a straight face—kept his cool and commanded the show. The people said Polk deserved such treatment for having harassed poor Cannon so a few years before.

Jones defeated Polk, but the conflict between the two parties continued over the issue of internal improvements. The Whigs felt the Democrats were giving work contracts to buy votes, or rather to influence elections, and that the state bank was being used for like purposes. So great was the discord that it carried over to the United States Congress.

The Whigs had a very small majority in the Tennessee House of Representatives in 1841. There were twelve Whigs and twelve Democrats in the state senate, plus one independent member; and there were two United States senators to be elected. The Independent, Samuel Turney, was elected speaker of the senate, and he and the twelve Democrats voted for H. L. Turney, Samuel's brother, for United States senator. (Samuel Turney and the twelve Democrats—Andrew Johnson was one of them—were called the "immortal thirteen.") The Whigs were unhappy over this situation and refused to accept it. They invited the Senate to meet them in joint session, but the Democrats refused. As a result of the conflict, the state was without senators in Washington from 1841 to 1843.

The state bank was causing so much trouble in the

state that Governor Jones nominated a new board of directors for it; but the immortal thirteen voted against them, leaving the Democrats in office. Jones then recommended an investigation of the affairs of the bank, but the immortal thirteen defeated this proposal as well. The Whigs were indignant and the populace grew suspicious that something indeed was "rotten in Democratic territory" and refused to vote for Polk who was running again for governor. Jones was reelected for a second term.

Although the Jones administration was stormy where the state bank was concerned, political bedlam was not totally supreme. The legislature of 1843 made two appropriations of lasting credit to the Jones administration: they gave the first money ever taken from the treasury for such a purpose to establish a school for the blind in Nashville, and a school for the deaf in Knoxville.

Jimmy Jones was born in Davidson County on June 7, 1809. His parents were Peter and Catherine Chapell Jones. Orphaned at an early age, he was left to the care of an uncle who did not stress education, though Jones did study in the Old Field Schools. In 1829 he married Sarah Munford of English-Welsh descent. She was the daughter of William and Letitia Ball Munford, and her grandfather had been a member of the Virginia House of Burgesses.

Jones was a farmer in Wilson County when he was elected to the legislature in 1837 and again in 1839. Like others of his day, he had read law on his own in his initial climb into politics, and had proved himself on the stump. And even though his own education was limited, he noted the importance of learning, deeming colleges and academies more reliable then the military where the welfare of the nation was concerned.

Jones' period in the governor's chair was a grand time in history, not only in Tennessee, but over the entire land. The people were caught up in the flourish of progress, for railroad locomotives had come to the world. The "iron horse in harness" speeding miraculously over the ground, anchored to the earth on beds of steel, was as spectacular an event for its day as Neil Armstrong's "giant step for mankind" when he lightly set foot on the moon in the twentieth century. The first train had made its exhibition run over the Lagrange and Memphis Railroad, and soon tunnels were pushed through the mountains to join Chattanooga and Nashville, Huntsville, Alabama, and other parts of the South. The public paraded through the tunnels with torches and lanterns held high, proclaiming this new day for their own. Now they could travel all the way to New Orleans by rail, whereas before only the river had sufficed as a transport.

Religious movements grew too, and the Methodist Episcopal Church and the Southern Baptist Convention evolved.

Nashville became the permanent state capital under the Jones administration, even though it had been used as the seat of the state legislature since 1826, during Governor Carroll's administration. The cornerstone of the capitol was laid in 1845, but the building was not finished until 1856.

When his second term in office expired, Jones declined to become a gubernatorial candidate again. He moved to Memphis to take over the presidency of the Memphis and Charleston Railroad, but the political life still held him under its spell. Jones returned to Nashville to run for a place in the United State Senate, and won the race. He served from March 4, 1851, until March 3, 1857. At his retirement, he returned to his home in Memphis where he died at age fifty, on October 29, 1859. He was buried in Elmwood Cemetery there, leaving his forty-seven-year-old widow and nine children. Jones was the first native son to fill the Tennessee governor's chair.

AARON VAIL BROWN
(Democrat)
(1845-1847)

From a pioneer's adobe-stripped log cabin to an ante-bellum governor's mansion is quite a step in one lifetime, but Aaron ("Fat") Brown made it.

Brunswick County, Virginia, contributed greatly to the populating of Tennessee as the early settlers pressed west-ward beyond the mountains, and Brown was among its contributions, being born there on August 15, 1795. His father was Aaron V., Sr., a Methodist minister, and his mother was Elizabeth Melton of North Hampton, North Carolina. Elizabeth was the minister's second wife, and bore him eight children; there were three others by the first marriage.

In 1813, the Brown family moved to Giles County, while young Aaron stayed behind to study law at the University of North Carolina. He was graduated in 1814 as valedictorian of his class, and then came to Tennessee to join his parents.

After further study of law in the office of James Trimble in Nashville, Brown entered a partnership with James Polk in Giles County, their firm serving not only that county but several surrounding ones. Brown was a handsome, sagacious young lawyer, and soon became well known throughout the area. When Polk entered Congress, the firm was dissolved, but Brown had made his mark in Tennessee. He served in the state senate from 1821 to 1827 (except in 1825); then in 1831 and again in 1833, he represented Giles County in the lower house of the legis-lature. Humanitarian in thought, the loquacious Brown let his concern for other human beings be known. He favored limiting the application of capital punishment and at the legislative session of 1831-32 prepared a report on that subject for the judiciary committee which attracted favorable attention in the state. Among the subheads of the document were such titles as "The Origin of Human Laws" and "The Right as Supposed to be Founded on Divine Revelation."

Such concern for society and world affairs boosted Brown to Congress by 1839 where he served continuously until 1845. He participated in the fiery debates of his time, and was a member of the committee that framed the Tariff of 1842, even though he had been among the minority that disapproved the bill.

With his service in Congress ending when Polk became president, Brown determined to devote himself to his personal affairs. Before he reached his home from Washington, however, he learned that the Democratic party in Tennessee had nominated him for governor in opposition to Ephraim H. Foster, the Whig candidate. Foster, a former senator, was one of the most able men of the Whig party, and Brown hesitated to accept the challenge. The Whig strength had not yet been broken in Tennessee; and President Polk, in reorganizing his administration, had selected some of the most powerful men in the Democratic party to fill the positions, drawing them out of state. So Brown was somewhat skeptical when he hesitantly agreed to run for the high office. But his fears were needless: he won the election by about 1,500 votes (He would be defeated by about half that number of votes in the next election, however, when the Whigs were to win.)

So evenly balanced were the political parties in Tennessee between the years of 1839, the year of Brown's inauguration, and 1853, when Andrew Johnson was elected, that the governors were alternately Democrats and Whigs, and none except James C. Jones held the office for more than one term.

One month after becoming governor, Brown married

James Chamberlain Jones
1841-1845

Neill S. Brown
1847-1849

Aaron Vail Brown
1845-1847

William Trousdale
1849-1851

for the second time. His first wife, who died when she was thirty-five, leaving six children for Brown to rear, had been Sarah Woodford Burrus, daughter of the eminent Judge Burrus of Amherst County, Virginia. The Burrus family was of Dutch-Irish descent, and the judge had left a family of fourteen children, many of them to become active in the political history of Tennessee. Governor Brown's children from this union kept up the tradition— one of the daughters married the grandson of Willie (Wylie) Blount, an early governor of the state, and a granddaughter became the mother of Hill McAlister, governor in 1933.

Governor Brown's second wife was Cynthia Pillow Saunders, the widow of John W. Saunders and the daughter of General Gideon J. Pillow. Gideon Pillow, a former lawyer in Nashville, was a brigadier general in the War with Mexico, a rank he retained as a Confederate officer during the Civil War. When he had moved to Maury County as a young man, he had bought 5,000 acres of land from General Nathanael Greene. On this site Pillow built a large home in Columbia, and it was here that his daughter Cynthia grew up, far removed from the pioneer days past. It was a time when those men who had bought up the new land for a few cents an acre could prosper, building enormous estates that remain today on the rich farming land in Middle Tennessee.

But Governor Brown was initiated to the antebellum atmosphere of the stately mansions when he married Mrs. Saunders. He moved his family to the Nashville estate, "Melrose," which had been given to Cynthia by her father when she became the bride of John W. Saunders. (Brown was the second governor to marry while in office; Houston had been the first.) There was no gubernatorial mansion in Nashville yet, but the widow's home with its winding drive from the entrance gate, set beyond its bordered gardens and marble fountain, made an ideal one. Here, among lovely furnishings and the finest collection of paintings in the United States at the time, lavish and frequent entertaining took place, and notables of every section of the South were entertained. Here, too, in the mansion, an only son was born to Governor and Mrs. Brown.

The first lady was a beautiful and charming hostess, and her graces won the approval of President James Buchanan, a bachelor, who called upon her to preside in the White House at social gatherings when the governor was later appointed to postmaster general in Washington.

Aaron Brown's administration, aside from political strife, was vexed with the heat of war. The annexation of Texas to the Union had occurred about the same time that he became governor, and danger of war had grown out of a dispute between Texas and Mexico over their boundry line. Texas claimed that the Rio Grand River was the line while Mexico insisted it was the Nueces River.The result of the argument was war which closed with the surrender of the city of Mexico to the United States in 1847.

Governor Brown called for 2,600 soldiers to help fight the Mexican War, and 30,000 answered. Tennessee had earned its epithet as the Volunteer State under Willie Blount, and indeed it would remain so. Among the famous Tennesseans who took part in the war were Gideon Pillow. W. T. Haskell, William B. Campbell, B. F. Cheatam, and William B. Tate. The fighting men of the state had been aroused by the treatment that Mexicans had given Tennesseans during the Texan Revolution of 1836—the latter had surrendered under a positive promise to be treated as prisoners of war, but instead, were murdered, among them the immortalized Davy Crockett.

The Mexican War, under a Tennessee president (Polk),

had resulted in the largest addition of land ever made to the United States, with the exception of the purchase of Louisiana under President Jefferson. But the acquisition increased the already existing strife regarding Negro slavery—would the new territory be slave or free? In Tennessee the people charged the struggles to the Democrats. Polk had been accused of being partial to the Democrats in making appointments, and of unfair treatment to Whig members. Governor Brown had to answer to the political accusations as well as controversies that grew out of the Mexican War, and by 1847, the people were ready for a Whig candidate. Aaron Brown left office after serving only one term.

Later, the ex-governor was appointed postmaster general by President Buchanan and moved his family to Washington; there Brown died of pneumonia on March 8, 1859. He was buried in Mt. Olive Cemetery in Nashville. Mrs. Brown and their children returned to Melrose.

N E I L L S. B R O W N
(Whig)
(1847-1849)

The Whigs' candidate for the gubernatorial election in 1847 was Neill S. (Lean) Brown of Giles County. He was born in 1810 the son of Duncan and Margaret Smith Brown. Both parents were of Scotch-Irish descent, and had moved to Giles County from North Carolina in 1809. Duncan Brown, a farmer, had been a Whig since the organization of that party, and possessed a good intellect, though he was evidently uneducated. Neill Brown's grandfather, Angus Brown, whose parents were emigrants from Scotland, had served in the Revolutionary War and was a true man of the soil. He was a strong Presbyterian of the old school, respected for his fairness and citizenship.

Neill Brown had inherited his father's and his grandfather's strong intellect, and though uneducated as a child,
decided at age seventeen that he wanted to be. He ventured
upon a mastery of the printed word on his own, studying by
a pine knot fire. After acquiring a limited education in this
area, Brown began teaching school in Giles County. His
teaching financed his college education, and after earning
that, he entered a study of law in 1833 at Pulaski.

Neill Brown was admitted to the bar at the close of
1834 and opened his own office in Pulaski. Later, he ventured to Texas with the thought of opening a law office;
but the probabilty of a lucrative practice there seemed
nonexistent, so he returned to Tennessee. In 1836 he
enlisted in the Seminole War, entering as a private, but
soon was promoted to sergeant major of his regiment,
the First Tennessee.

A fine prospect for a political Whig figure, Brown
was nominated by the party as an elector at large for
Hugh Lawson White, candidate for the presidency in 1837.
In that election, and in the two successive presidential
contests, Brown took the stump for the Whig candidates,
campaigning for Harrison in 1840 and for Henry Clay in
1844. Such rhetoric as Brown's was not to be overlooked
by Tennesseans, and they sent him to the state legislature
where he served six years; in 1847 they elected him
governor.

Meanwhile, he had married Mary Ann Trimble, daughter of Judge James Trimble of Nashville, whose law office
had been a part of the young governor's education. Mrs.
Brown's mother was Letitia Breckenridge Clark. Mary
Brown, like the governor's ancestors, was a strong Presbyterian with her own keen intellect, and shared her husband's interest in the Whig party.

Neill Brown's administration was a time of change,
coupled with the inevitable political excitement. The first

telegraph company was established in Tennessee, chartered by the New Orleans and Ohio Telegraph Co., and the first dispatched telegraph, appropriately enough, announced the victory of Whig candidate Zachary Taylor in the presidential election returns of 1848. The state formed its first historical society. One of Governor Brown's greatest contributions to the state was his effort to develop a public school system. Recalling the pine knot flicker in his own printed page, he urged the legislature to establish public schools. An act was passed, but implementation depended on the counties and no permanent system resulted.

The year following Taylor's election as president, the party again nominated Neill Brown for governor, and he sharpened up his wit for the podium. But now it was the Democrats' turn at the realm of state government, and their candidate, William Trousdale, was elected.

But the Whigs were not yet finished with the talented ex-governor. In 1850, President Taylor commissioned Brown minister to Russia, where he remained for three years. Mrs. Brown and the children, who lived at their "Idlewood" estate in Nashville, visited him for a while, and then returned by boat to Nashville.

After his own return to Nashville in 1853, Brown was sent in 1855 to the lower house of the legislature from Davidson County, and was elected speaker. He was an active and influential member of the constitutional convention of 1879, and then took no further part in politics. The Whigs had acknowledged him as one of the greatest Whig leaders, and history records him as one of the purest of public figures.

He took no official part in the War between the States, but sympathized with the Confederates. And like many other Southerners who suffered at the expense of battle, the Browns lost their home in a fire set by the federal soldiers.

Neill Brown's devotion to politics prevented his full development as a lawyer, a profession for which he had great potential. He seemed to have regretted this fact in his later life, and expressed some despair concerning it, feeling that he should have given more of his time to his work rather than to the stump. For words, flung in the wind, are at best short-lived, no matter how elocutive.

Passing his last years in tranquil retirement, he died on January 30, 1886, and was buried in Mount Olivet Cemetery in Nashville; his widow died in 1895. Eight children had been born to their union, and the Browns lived through the death of four of their sons.

WILLIAM TROUSDALE
(Democrat)
(1849-1851)

William Trousdale was known as the "War Horse of Sumner County." He belonged to that gallant group of Tennesseans who stood ready to fight at the drop of a hat, provided they believed in the cause.

Trousdale was born in Orange County, North Carolina, in 1790, and came to Tennessee when he was six years old. His parents, James and Elizabeth Dobbins Trousdale, of Scotch-Irish descent, had settled in North Carolina before the Revolutionary War. Later, the family moved on westward, settling in Sumner County the year that the Territory South of the River Ohio became the state of Tennessee.

James Trousdale had been a captain in the Revolutionary War, and he received a land grant in 1784 in connection with his military services. This grant took in a large area of land that was to become the present site of Gallatin, but then it was the family farm.

In 1801 the legislature of Tennessee appointed com-

missioners to locate an area for the county seat of Sumner
County. The committee chose the Trousdale farm, which
was broken up into lots and established as the county seat.
(A huge family mansion, through the ownership of Governor Trousdale's son, has become a notable state land-
mark under the auspices of the United Daughters of the
Confederacy.)

Sure that "book learning" could not compare with the
excitement of war, young William left the Sumner County
area schools—feeble enough at that—to fight in the Creek
War. He was with Andrew Jackson at Pensacola, and won
fame as a fighter in the Mexican War. Twice wounded in
battle, he was promoted to brigadier-general in the United
States Army as a result of his courageous crusades. During
one campaign, he swam his horse across the Tennessee
River, though it is recorded that he couldn't swim a stroke
himself. But such daring escapades earned him his celebrated title.

Trousdale married Mary Ann Bugg, daughter of Samuel
and Frances Lewis Bugg, who had come into the state
from Mecklenburg County, Virginia, and settled in Sumner
County as well.

Before his notable activity with the army, Trousdale
had served in the state senate in 1835. His political experience and military exploits seemed to appeal to Tennesseans; in the 1849 gubernatorial election, he defeated incumbent governor Neill Brown by some 1,400 votes.

The most significant event of Trousdale's administration was the assembling of the Southern Convention in
Nashville in 1850 to discuss the slavery question. Langdon
Cheves of South Carolina and other strong secession
leaders of the lower South were in charge of the meeting,
which over 100 Tennesseans attended after the Whig-
dominated legislature defeated efforts of the Democrats to
elect "official" delegates. The Whigs had not wanted the

convention held in Nashville in the first place, asserting that Tennessee should not be a stomping ground for seceders and nullifiers and urged the "plotters" to assemble elsewhere.

The Democrats, however, were in favor of Tennessee's hosting the convention that had grown out of controversy over the Wilmot Proviso, a proposal that would exclude slaveholders from the newly gained lands in Texas for which Southerners had fought. State senators in Tennessee agreed unanimously that they were opposed to the measure in "every shape and form." President Polk conceded that the Proviso was a "mischievous and foolish amendment," and Andrew Johnson himself looked at the measure from the Southerners' point of view.

Hence the convention members were ready to denounce Northern abolitionists, deem the Wilmot Proviso unconstitutional, and demand that a stringent fugitive slave law be enacted. The Southern Convention wanted the Mexican territory divided along the Missouri Compromise line, and declared that until some agreement was reached, all states had a right to the new land.

But it was Henry Clay, still an idol of Tennesseeans, who would introduce proposals in Washington that would eventually result in the Compromise of 1850, which would end sectionalism to some degree, and most Tennesseeans acted in good faith toward it. In a second session of the Southern Convention held in November, Aaron V. Brown, former governor of the state, helped to draft a resolution urging that "all Americans, regardless of their feelings, should strive to bind up the nation's wounds and preserve the Union and the Constitution."[5]

But the general populace could not be so objective. Willingness of the Democrats to accept the sudden change

[5]Stanley J. Folmsbee, Robert E. Corlew, and Enoch Mitchell, *Tennessee: A Short History* (Knoxville: University of Tennessee Press, 1972), 230.

of pace seemed suspicious to some, and Trousdale, who had been nominated for governor again, lost his place to William B. Campbell.

In 1852, President Franklin Pierce made Trousdale minister to Brazil. He died on March 27, 1872, and was buried in Gallatin.

WILLIAM BOWEN CAMPBELL
(Whig)
(1851-1853)

The Whig party was dying out in Tennessee during the early 1850s, and William Campbell would be the last Whig governor. He was the third native son to hold the high office. In the presidential election of 1853, the Whigs carried the state for their candidate, General Winfield Scott, but the Democratic candidate, Franklin Pierce, was elected president. This was the last election in which the Whigs carried the state.

It was still a great time in history for the politician, and the Democratic governor, William Trousdale, ran again in opposition to Campbell. Both men canvassed the state, but this campaign was conducted in a different pattern from the spectacular expositions of the past. The two candidates were brilliant men, and gentlemen, and left off the back-biting debates addressing one another in as "courteous a manner as if they had been speaking in a parlor, with ladies for an audience."[6]

Campbell stood high in the state's history already, having pushed his way up from his father's farm, which had proved unsuccessful. He was born to David and Catherine Bowen Campbell on February 1, 1807, on Manker's Creek in Sumner County. His ancestors were of

[6]Gentry R. McGee, *A History of Tennessee* (Nashville: Charles Elder, facsimile reproduction, 1971), 173.

Lancaster County, Pennsylvania, pioneer stock who had pushed on into Virginia and then into Tennessee. William was the oldest of six children, and when his father's farm failed, the youth was sent to Abingdon, Virginia, where he completed his education under his uncle, the governor of Virginia.

Young Campbell studied law in his uncle's law office, and then returned to Tennessee to establish his own practice in Carthage about 1829. Soon thereafter he became attorney for the state, and in 1835 he was elected to the legislature by Smith County. But he resigned his position in the legislature to enter the army and was named captain of a group of volunteers for the Seminole War where he established a reputation for his courage and skill. Commanding the regiment in which Campbell served was General William Trousdale, the War Horse, the same man whom Campbell would oppose in a congressional race in 1837 and would unseat from the governor's chair.

Campbell won the congressional seat from Trousdale as well, and he served three terms, after which he returned to private practice in law. But when Governor Aaron Brown appealed for Tennessee troops for the Mexican War in 1846, Campbell was among the 30,000 who volunteered. He was made colonel for a group of Middle Tennessee volunteer soldiers called the First Regiment of Tennessee Volunteers.

Campbell and his men showed their bravery in the Mexican War at the Battle of Monterey which was fought in September of 1846. Leaving to assist General Taylor in the fight, the regiment went by steamboat to New Orleans, then by sailing vessels across the Gulf of Mexico, and on by steamers up the Rio Grande to Camargo. The general's troops of 6,000 men were raw and undisciplined, and they undertook to capture a city fortified by twice their number of men. The First Tennessee was the first regiment to enter the city and to raise the American flag within its walls, losing one-third of the battalion's men in the effort. In his charge to enter the city, Colonel Campbell echoed Sevier's bold command, "Boys, follow me!"

The charge became famous throughout the American army and added to the already gallant reputation of Tennessee soldiers. Thereafter, the First Tennessee Regiment was known as the "Bloody First" and was transferred from General Taylor's army to the command of General Scott at Vera Cruz where Colonel Campbell was closely associated with General Robert E. Lee. The Bloody First was active in various battles for the following year and was then sent home to be mustered out, its record perpetuated forever in the annals of Tennessee history.

Consequently, when Campbell ran for the gubernatorial race, Tennesseans had their minds made up. The colonel won handily. As governor, he was fair and capable; but as with other soldiers in the state's records, his image as a fighter overrides that of high executive. At the end of one term, Campbell declined to run for office a second time, intending to give his attention to private affairs.

Meanwhile, in 1835, he had married Frances Isabella Owen, the daughter of Dr. John and Mary Goodwin Owen of Smith County. Nine children were born to their union. They had first made their home in Carthage, but in 1853 the ex-governor moved his family to Lebanon, where he had accepted the presidency of the Bank of Middle Tennessee.

During the turmoil of 1861, when a part of the state's populace wanted to stay with the Union and the other part wanted to withdraw, Campbell canvassed the state in opposition to secession. An outspoken supporter of the Union, he had been offered the command of all the Tennessee forces that could be raised for the Confederate army, but declined that leadership. In May, 1862, he was unanimously chosen president of a mass meeting of federal supporters held at Nashville which urged Tennesseans to return the state to the Union.

On July 23, 1862, the ex-governor accepted the office of brigadier general in the federal army with the understanding that he not be assigned to duty in the field. He accepted this position with the hope that he might serve as peacemaker between the government of the United States and the people of Tennessee. But he resigned the post the following month, resolving that he would never draw his sword against Tennesseans, even though he believed them to be wrong in seceding from the Union.

Campbell had allied himself with the Democratic party by the time Andrew Johnson became military governor of the state following the Civil War; but he opposed Johnson's procedures in regulating elections among the people, and the opposition produced a breech between them. Their differences were mended, however, after Johnson became president of the United States by succession, following President Lincoln's assassination.

In 1865, William Campbell was elected to the Thirty-ninth Congress. In the heated raucourous debates of that session regarding impeachment charges against Johnson, Campbell was a staunch defender of the president. After Johnson's impeachment, Campbell remained in Washington throughout the impeachment trial. He was constantly at Johnson's side as one of his trusted advisors.

Campbell's appointment to Congress was his last political position. After his service there, he retired to his home in Lebanon , where he died on August 19, 1867. He was buried in Cedar Grove Cemetery at Lebanon. Mrs. Campbell had died three years earlier.

ANDREW JOHNSON
(Democrat)
(1853-1857; 1862-1865)

The life of Andrew Johnson is little less than legend where the poor-boy-makes-good motif is concerned, only overshadowed by Lincoln's. Though the two climbed their ladders of success separately, they walked similar paths, and were ironically thrown together in working out the problems of a troubled land following the Civil War.

Like Lincoln, Johnson was born in poverty. Arriving in the world at the "poor white" class stratum, he worked his way up to the highest office in the country with hardly any help other than his own initiative. As he walked along, covered with dust, behind the one-horse cart that brought his mother and stepfather across the Allegheny Mountains into Tennessee, it hardly seemed conceivable that the strong shouldered, stubby legged youth with a mass of sticky black hair falling across his brow would one day serve the state as governor, much less fill the presidency of the United States.

He was born in the town of Raleigh, North Carolina, on December 29, 1808, to an illiterate drifter from England, Jacob Johnson, and his wife, Mary McDonough Johnson. When Andrew was three, his father died, and his mother supported him and his older brother by taking in washing and sewing.

Mary Johnson married a second husband, Turner Dougherty, but he did not prove to be a breadwinner. Barely able to feed her sons, let alone send them to school, Mrs. Dougherty allowed them to roam the streets where they were recognized as common mudsills. Whether to give them a better life, or to avoid the weight of responsibility, she apprenticed them to James Shelby, the town tailor, where they were to be indentured until the age of twenty-one.

Isham Green Harris
1857-1862

William Bowen Campbell
1851-1853

Robert Looney Caruthers
1863

Andrew Johnson
1853-1857, 1862-1865

It was the custom in that day for the tailors to hire someone to read to the young learners as they cut and sewed material, and the employee who read to Andrew started him on a thirst for knowledge that was never quenched. He was thrilled by the printed words and learned to piece them together on a page, teaching himself to read.

Dissatisfied with their bondage, the boys ran away from their master. The older brother continued on in his search for greener pastures; but after a few months, Andrew's conscience got the best of him and he returned to Raleigh, intending to pay his forfeiture of indenture to the veteran tailor who had taught him a trade. Shelby had discontinued his tailoring business by that time, however, so Andrew put up his own shop.

At age seventeen, Andrew assumed the role of leader in his family and made the decision to move his mother and irresponsible stepfather beyond the mountains into Tennessee. The family settled in Greenville in the eastern part of the state, and there Andrew again set up a tailor shop. In 1827 he married Eliza McCardle, a schoolteacher in the area who taught him to write and to do mathematic sums. Still enthralled by the printed page, he borrowed books from the college library in Greenville and furthered his education. Discovering that he had a gift for oratory, he joined a debating group at the college, and walked four miles to join in the weekly debates.

Johnson was disturbed that the power of government belonged to the aristocracy and started voicing his personal political views. Soon, his tailor's shop was the meeting place for the civic-minded common men who elected him first alderman in their town and then mayor. Having whetted his appetite with the taste of civil leadership, he now aspired to the legislature, and was elected to the Tennessee House of Representatives in 1835.

While in the legislature, Johnson continued to work on his education, borrowing grammar books to study sentence structure; but his speeches were not written out. Rather, he researched his subjects well and spoke from his heart, and his simple down-to-earth vernacular reached the ordinary people who were filling the state of Tennessee. He voted for what he felt was right and spoke his opinion when he felt the need to, making enemies of the large landowners. Many of his proposals, opposed at the time, have since been accepted as sound by authorities in government, such as the twentieth-century clamor regarding prayer and Bible-reading in the schools.

Although Johnson was not irreligious, he proposed a bill that denounced the opening of the legislature with prayer because he felt that church and state should be kept entirely separate. The act cost him a part of his following among the nineteenth-century pious. That proposal perhaps, coupled with his opposition against a bill for internal improvements in the state because the measure would instigate graft, lost him the election in 1837. But his prophecy on the latter issue proved true, and the voters sent him back to the legislature in 1839.

In 1841 Johnson was elected to the state senate, and by 1843 had won a seat in the Congress of the United States, becoming the recognized political leader of Eastern Tennessee. Ever conscious of the grinding poverty of his childhood, he kept the poor within his political vision. He proposed a Homestead Act (on which he worked twenty years before it was finally passed in 1862) wherein any man who was the head of a family and a citizen of the United States would be entitled to 160 acres if he would move to the land, build his home there, and cultivate the soil for five years. This bill would have made federal lands available to poor white settlers and destroyed slavery. Although Johnson himself was a slaveowner, he was against slavery, and fought the "Three-Fifths Clause" in Tennessee's constitution that allowed a proportionate number of votes to be cast by slaveholders in accordance with the number of slaves they owned.

Johnson's opponent saw to it in 1853 that his congressional district was rearranged, giving the Whigs a majority vote in the following election. He knew that he would lose his seat in Congress, so he resigned his position and ran for governor of Tennessee, winning the election. Hating fanfare and extravagance, he refused the gala inaugural parade that his friends had planned for him. Instead, he walked to the capitol (as he did every day thereafter as governor), took a handful of rumpled notes from his pocket, and delivered his address.

The Nashville elite dubbed the governor as uncouth, the common tailor risen above his station in life, but even so, Johnson remained undaunted in his effort to serve the state well. He proposed the first statewide tax to support schools, outlined plans to refinance the state debt and reform the banking and penal systems, and proposed speeding up work of the courts to avoid expense and delays in waiting for court decisions.

In an effort to encourage better farming, a bureau of agriculture was established and the first state fairs were started so that the farmer could display his products and the smithy could show his wares. More railroads were built with state backing during Johnson's administration than during any previous administration, and the material and cultural growth of the state bounded forward. The Tennessee Historical Society was permanently organized at Nashville in 1857, though it had been instituted at an earlier date. Before the reign of Johnson, the state library was composed almost entirely of court papers and documents, but in 1854 the legislature appropriated $5,000 to buy books for the library and hired the first state librarian. For his entire first term in office Johnson looked away from national politics, giving his attention to state affairs.

The following election year did not go smoothly for him. Johnson again sought the governorship, but was opposed by both the Whigs and the Know-Nothing party. At one public meeting he was threatened with assassination; but, without a bodyguard, he faced his audience, fingered the pistol on his hip, and dared anyone who so desired to attack him. No one did, and he was reelected governor.

Ill health due to an injury from a train accident deemed Johnson unsuitable to be greatly involved in politics that following election year, so the party convention nominated Isham Harris as the Democratic choice to succeed him as governor. But Johnson was not yet finished with politics. By October he was on his feet once more, and returned to Washington in 1857 as the United States senator from Tennessee.

It was a troublesome time for the South, torn apart by the Civil War. Johnson took a firm stand on holding the Union together, opposing the secession of the southern states from it. But the South refused to hear his voice. When, against his protest, Tennessee did withdraw from the Union, he remained in Congress, the only senator who refused to secede with his state.

President Lincoln appointed him military governor of Tennessee in 1862. Johnson's plans were to lead the state back into the Union. He advocated allowing free elections for the voters who would take an oath against the rebellion and accept the Emancipation Proclamation, provided those voters had not supported the Confederacy. His plan succeeded and by March of 1864 Tennessee was again making plans to send representatives to Congress.

Johnson's devotion to the Union and his record as military governor of Tennessee made him a national figure, and he was elected as Lincoln's vice-president in 1865. Therefore a Republican president and a Democratic vice-president worked out a reconstruction program for a disturbed South that was attempting recovery from the Civil War. Johnson was hailed by the North as a patriot, and branded by his Southern colleagues as a traitor.

On April 15, 1865, Lincoln was assassinated, and Johnson found himself president of the United States, only six weeks after his inauguration as vice-president. The War between the States was just coming to an end, and now the awesome task of carrying through the reconstruction program initiated by Lincoln was at hand. Johnson sought to carry it to the finish. In the final outcome, he found himself and his motives misunderstood. In calling for the resignation of Edwin M. Stanton, secretary of war, Johnson was charged with violating the Tenure-of-Office Act—supposedly ruled unconstitutional by the Supreme Court in 1926—a bill preventing the president from removing officeholders confirmed by the Senate without their consent. He was attacked by his Congress, and in an action unequaled until the twentieth-century Watergate, was faced with impeachment.

In an effort to remove Johnson from office, the House of Representatives brought eleven charges against him. The country grew tired of the proceedings in Washington where the punitive measures against the president were overshadowed by the spectacular behavior of the Radical orators. He did not appear at his trial; William Evarts of New York defended him. The convicting vote fell one short of the two-thirds majority necessary for impeachment; that vote was cast by Edmund Ross, a Republican (Whig) senator from Kansas.

The Democratic party did not nominate Johnson as their candidate for the presidency in 1868. They chose instead Horatio Seymour of New York. When Johnson's term in the White House was finished, he and his family returned to their old home in Greeneville. The state returned him to the Senate in 1875, the first time in the history of the United States that a former president was elected to the Senate.

Andrew Johnson died from a paralytic stroke on July 31, 1875, and was buried at Greeneville. Within a year his wife Eliza, who had been an invalid in her later years, was buried beside him. They left two daughters; three sons had preceded them in death.

Twentieth-century thinkers have defended "the common tailor risen above his station" as a wise leader, and have categorized his intellect, that so nearly missed its fulfillment, with that of Jackson and Lincoln.

ISHAM GREEN HARRIS
(Democrat)
(1857-1862)

Isham Green Harris was the fourth Tennessee governor born and reared in that state, and the first governor from West Tennessee. His public career covered a span of fifty years, the greater part of that time being the most turbulent and bloodiest period the nation has ever known.

The third generation to bear the name of Isham Green, Harris was the youngest of nine children born to Isham Green and Lucy Davidson Harris. Grandfather Isham, like so many others of his day, was of Revolutionary and North Carolina stock.

The Harris family, as the other pioneers, desired fresher fields and pressed westward over the mountains, settling near Tullahoma where the waters of Elk River

flowed through a valley overlooked by the Cumberland
Mountains. Isham was born there on February 10, 1818.
He received the average education of a boy in his area,
remaining in school until about fifteen years of age, even
though his desire was to study law. But Isham's father was
poor in health, and the family farm—its livelihood—
suffered. So young Harris went to West Tennessee, living
near an older brother who had become a prosperous
lawyer in Paris. There he took a job as a clerk in a store,
earning $100 a year and his board.

Always the watcher, he learned the mercantile business
well, and within a short while convinced his brother to
back him in a business of his own. With borrowed money,
Isham went to Ripley, Mississippi, and opened a business.
In less that two years, while his business was showing a
worthwhile profit, he sold it. With money in his pocket, he
returned to Middle Tennessee, paid off the mortgage on his
father's farm, and then sold the property. He moved his
parents to Paris, where he bought a home for them in
Henry County. (At their deaths, they left all they owned
to this fine son, hoping to repay him for his care of them.
But the gallant Isham would have no such familial par-
tiality. Instead, he called his brothers together and convinced them that their sisters should have the property.
Isham tore up the will and left another, passing the
property to his sisters.)

Now in his early thirties, Harris borrowed more money
and went into business a second time. He had not given up
his desire to study law, however; and by 1841 he had
climbed that mountain too, and had become a practicing
attorney.

He was as successful at law as at business, and by 1847
he had been elected senator for Henry, Weakley, and
Obion counties (the three counties shared one senator).
Harris was elected to the state house of representatives in

1849 and reelected in 1851. In 1853 he declined to run again and moved to Memphis to practice law.

Meanwhile, he had married Martha Travis in 1843. She was the daughter of Major Edward and Martha Blanton Travis of Henry County. Her paternal grandparents were Colonel Edward Champion and Booth Travis of Virginia.

After moving to Memphis, Harris did not reappear in public life until 1856, when he was named elector for the state at large, campaigning for Buchanan. In 1857 he defeated Robert Hatton, Whig candidate, in the race for governor by a majority of 11,000 votes. The two had canvassed the state in the usual manner, carrying on heated debates, but they had differences along the trail and cut their campaign short, much to the regret of the speech-loving Tennesseans.

Harris found himself in the governor's chair at a time when the eyes of all Southerners seemed upon him. He was a determined and energetic individual, popular with the people. But circumstances often make or break the man, and Harris has been both applauded and castigated in the annals of Tennessee's history because of his position at that crucial time. The South was nearing the Civil War. The Whig party was on its way to extinction, and the Democrats were sweeping the country. In the previous election (1856) the state had given its electoral votes to James Buchanan—the first time Tennessee had voted for a Democratic candidate for president since the election of Andrew Jackson in 1832. And national leader that the state had become, the southern states looked now to see what its position would be in regard to Lincoln and the presidential election of 1860.

Secession from the Union was on every tongue, and Harris, a firm supporter of states' rights, tried to lead Tennessee toward it. As soon as the other southern states began seceding from the Union, he assembled the state legislature, asking that a resolution be passed requesting the people to vote on the 9th of February, 1861, for or against secession. All of Tennessee was not in sympathy with the Confederate South, however, and most of them clung to the desire to stand by the Union. The legislature voted against the proposition almost four to one.

When Lincoln went into office March 4, 1861, with his proclamation that the states should rule individually on the slavery issue, Tennesseans were generally pleased with their vote. But when, in April following, South Carolina soldiers attacked Fort Sumter in Charleston Harbor and forced the United States garrison to surrender the fort, Lincoln could no longer stick to his original strategy. He called for 75,000 soldiers to force the seceded states back under the authority of the Union. This meant war, and Tennesseans knew they were to be involved in it.

President Lincoln called for soldiers from Tennessee, but Governor Harris refused to send them, and said that if Tennessee must fight, then Tennessee would fight with the South. The legislature was called together for a second vote, and this time the vote for secession was more than two to one.

On July 2, Tennessee became the last state to secede, It joined South Carolina, Mississippi, Alabama, Florida, Georgia, Louisiana, and Texas as one of the Confederate States of America at Montgomery, Alabama, on February 4, 1861. A majority of the people of East Tennessee clung to the Union until the last, even petitioning the legislature to allow them to form a separate state, but the request was refused. The split in opinion resulted in split allegiance in some 30,000 fighting in the federal army and over 100,000 on the Confederate side.

In spite of the strife within the state, Governor Harris was reelected in the autumn of 1861 for his third term as governor. Although Robert L. Caruthers was elected in

1863, Harris remained nominally Tennessee's governor until the war ended, for Caruthers never took office. Andrew Johnson was appointed military governor of the state following the war, and Harris had to resign.

The federal army occupied Middle and West Tennessee in 1862, and Harris was forced to leave the state because of his Confederate stand. He became a volunteer member of the staffs of Albert Sidney Johnson, Braxton Bragg, and Joseph E. Johnston, and fought in every important battle of the war outside of Virginia except that of Perryville, Kentucky.

Following the war, Harris fled to Mexico. Brownlow, a Union supporter, had become the governor of Tennessee. He set a price on the ex-governor's head describing him thusly:

> His complexion is sallow. His eyes are dark and pene-trating—a perfect index to a heart of a traitor—with the scowl and frown of a demon resting upon his brow. His study of mischief and the practice of crime have brought upon him premature baldness and a gray beard. With brazen-faced impudence he talks loudly and boastingly of the overthrow of the Yankee Army, and entertains no doubt but that the South will achieve her independence. He chews tobacco rapidly and is inordinately fond of liquor. In his moral structure he is an unscrupulous man, steeped to the chin in personal and political profligacy—now about lost to all sense of shame, honor, with a heart reckless of social duty, and fatally bent upon mischief. If captured he will be found lurking in the Rebel strongholds of Alabama, Mississippi or Georgia and familiar society, alleging with the cheap-faced modesty of a virtuous man that it is not a wholesome state of public sentiment or of taste that forbids the indiscriminate mixing together of married men and women.[7]

Leaving his family in Mexico, Harris went to England for a couple of years until it was safe to return to Tennes-

[7] Kenneth McKallar, *Tennessee Senators* (Kingsport: Southern Publishers, 1942), 393.

see soil again. In 1867, he returned to Memphis and resumed his law practice. In spite of the controversy surrounding him, Tennesseans elected him to the United States Senate ten years later.

Even though his reign had been touched by the scars of war, Harris' administration had known cultural influences, too. He had strengthened the state library and historical society and made plans for use of the property left the state by Andrew Jackson, known as the Hermitage, which remains one of Tennessee's most famous historical sites.

Harris' main conflict with the people, aside from the fact that many blamed him for the rebellion, arose over his alleged theft of the common school fund. These monies had been deposited in the Bank of Tennessee, to be applied to education as the legislature directed. Such payments had continued until the Civil War, when they were removed from the bank; Harris was supposedly responsible for misplacing some $60,000 of this fund and fleeing the state with the money.

However in a publication on the first ladies of Tennessee, Nancy W. Walker stated that Mrs. Harris packed the missing school fund in her household goods when she moved her children (she was the mother of eight) to Mexico to join the exiled Harris there during the Brownlow administration.[8] According to Walker, the gold was stored in barrels all the while the ex-governor and his family lived in Mexico. At any rate, he reimbursed the state when he returned to take up his law practice, and insisted that the money had been removed for its safe-keeping during the war.

After his election to the Senate in 1876, Harris remained a strong political figure until his death at Washington in July, 1897. He was buried in Elmwood Cemetery at Memphis.

[8]Walker, *Out of a Clear Blue Sky*, 153.

ROBERT LOONEY CARUTHERS
(Republican)
(Elected 1863, never inaugurated)

Caruthers was Tennessee's governor without a government. He was elected to the office in 1863, following Governor Harris' chaotic reign; but because war had taken over the state and it had seceded from the Union, Andrew Johnson had been appointed by President Lincoln as military governor in the hope that he could lead Tennessee back into the Union. Therefore, Caruthers was never inaugurated, although he remained an influential member of the state's populace.

The Caruthers family was one of the oldest in Tennessee, the first of them coming to America from Scotland, and settling in Virginia and North Carolina. Taking the route of so many immigrants, they moved on into Tennessee and settled in Maury County near the Columbia area. Robert Looney's parents were Samuel and Jane Looney Caruthers, and he was the youngest of their seven children. He was born in Smith County, where he entered the area schools, finishing his education at Washington College in East Tennessee.

After reading law with Judge Samuel Powell at Greeneville, Caruthers began a law practice at Carthage, but soon afterwards moved to Lebanon in Wilson County. His political life started as a clerk in the lower house of the legislature that met in Murfreesboro in 1823. Sam Houston then appointed him state attorney for the Lebanon Circuit in 1827, a position he held for five years. Next, he went to the legislature to represent Wilson County; in this legislature, the first under the new state constitution, he became a member of the House Judiciary Committee, By 1841 he succeeded John Bell in Congress, but declined reelection there; he was an elector for the state at large for the Whig ticket in 1844, and found himself on the supreme court bench when Governor William B. Campbell appointed him to fill a vacancy created by Nathan Green in 1852. The legislature elected him to the same office the following year, and the people returned him to his same position in 1854 after the amendment to the constitution depriving the legislature of the power to elect judges. He remained on the bench until the court was suspended as a result of the war.

When Harris' third term as governor ended, Judge Caruthers was elected to succeed him, but the state was in the possession of contending armies, and he did not take the oath; Johnson was acting military governor.

In the same year that he was elected governor, Caruthers married Sarah Vaughn Lawrence, whose family had a large plantation in Davidson County. She had one son by her previous marriage, Vaughn, who had served with General Forrest during the Civil War and had been held prisoner by the federal authorities. Because of illness he was returned to his home, which burned to the ground shortly thereafter.

Caruthers himself was not engaged in the war; his health disqualified him from active service, but he was in sentiment with the Confederates, and served in the secret service of the Confederacy.

Caruthers was the first president of the board of trustees of Cumberland University (Presbyterian) at Lebanon and co-founder of the Cumberland University Law School. The establishment of a school of law as an outgrowth of a primary theological institute met with opposition among the Presbyterian laity until the trustees published a written pledge stating that the law school would be self-supporting, with no assistance from the church. Abraham Caruthers, brother to Robert Looney and his partner in founding the institution, served as the first professor of law there. The work and influence of these two men have left a lasting imprint in Tennessee jurisprudence.

Robert Caruthers died October 2, 1882, and was buried at Lebanon.

WILLIAM GANNAWAY BROWNLOW
(Whig)
(1865-1869)

Brownlow was governor of Tennessee during the reconstruction of the South. All that the war had torn away had to be replaced, when possible. Not only did property need to be restored, but emotional stability as well.

Andrew Johnson had been the military governor from 1862 until 1865, when he resigned to leave for Washington as vice-president to President Lincoln. The East Tennessee Unionism used the collapse of the Confederacy and the election of Lincoln as a strategic opportunity to return the state to civil government under Union rule. A committee calling itself the East Tennessee Central Committee met in Nashville in January, 1865 and transformed itself into a dictator, forming a constitutional convention that proceded to free Tennessee's slaves, repudiate the secession ordinances and all confederate debts, and provide for the election of a governor and legislature. This election was to take place on March 4, the day that Lincoln and Johnson were to be inaugurated. The convention nominated Parson Brownlow as candidate for governor and selected the entire legislative slate.

Confederate supporters and Union men were at one another's throats; fathers turned against sons and sons against fathers because of individual opinions regarding the war. Men either weighed themselves in the light of their own consciences and reacted according to convictions, or they were carried along by the stream of human emotion that follows traumatic events adding to the unrest and disharmony was the havoc caused by the homeless men who wandered over the country, rioting and ravishing as they pleased, and stealing what they would.

Over such conditions William Brownlow found himself administrator in 1865. No other man had been considered in the gubernatorial race. The newspapers were openly determined in their preference for the Methodist preacher turned politician. In spite of the fact that Brownlow was not considered by the conservative element in the state a suitable person to best help the state as a whole, over 23,000 voters (against 35) cast their votes for him.

A break in command developed when Johnson left the office on March 4, for Brownlow could not be inaugurated until the legislature convened in April. But the new governor declared himself king, lest another should take that initiative, and undertook to straighten out the plight in which the state found itself.

History lists his administration as the "regime of Parson Brownlow," one of the most remarkable records of Tennessee's governors. Hardly anything governmental was done without the governor's prior consent, and reports of actions in every part of the state were forwarded to him immediately after their occurrence. Records in the state library show letters to Brownlow from sheriffs of various counties and from friends with reports of crimes and rioting in their cities. Whether or not he could help the situations, Brownlow wanted a report on them.

William Brownlow was born in Wythe County, Virginia, on August 29, 1805, to Joseph and Catherine Cannaway Brownlow, of Scotch-Irish ancestry. He was left an orphan at the age of eleven and his opportunities for education were limited. At eighteen he went to Abingdon, where he learned carpentry; at night he studied on his own, applying himself as a novice journalist.

Giving up his trade as a carpenter for the ministry Brownlow was licensed to preach by the Methodist Episcopal Church, and mingled his doctrinal beliefs with his political philosophy in support of the Whig party. After coming into Tennessee in 1828, he became the minister in a local church at Jonesboro and established a Whig newspaper in Elizabethton, Tennessee. The publication, known first as the *Elizabethton Whig*, started its circulation in 1838. Later, the newspaper was printed in Jonesboro and called *Brownlow's Jonesboro Whig*; still later Knoxville became its headquarters, where it received distinction as *The Knoxville Whig*, creating strong sentiment for the Union and even stronger feeling for its editor.

In contrast to Harris before him, Brownlow was an intense Unionist. Although opposed to the Democratic party and a determined enemy of secession, he was at the same time an advocate of slavery, and at the close of the war strongly opposed giving former slaves the ballot. Openly defending the institution of slavery in debates, he was arrested for giving free rein to his opinion, and his newspaper was suppressed by the Confederates in 1861. Publication was started again in 1864 when the Union army took over Knoxville.

Other works for which the governor was responsible included *The Iron Wheel Examined* (1865), which contained the parson's reply to attacks on Methodism, *Sketches of the Rise, Progress, and Decline of Secession* (1862), and *Ought American Slavery Be Abolished?*, a debate with a minister in New York. But the most famous of his publications was one he called *Parson Brownlow's Book*. In this volume Brownlow recounted unpleasant experiences with the Confederates and set forth his views on secession and the war. He regarded secession as foolish and wicked.

Brownlow ran for Congress against Andrew Johnson in 1843, but was defeated in that race. A true Union man, he was a member of the convention that revised the constitution of the state, and was elected governor in 1865 and again in 1867.

As head of the reconstruction program in the state, Brownlow saw to it that all persons who had either directly or indirectly taken any part in opposing the federal government, or who had given aid to the Confederates, were not allowed to vote at any election. Such ruling would give the control of the state to a minority of the people. The legislature passed franchise acts which gave the governor unlimited power. Consequently, those who were not allowed to vote became defiant, and opposed the state government in every way possible. Such opposition strengthened the split among Union supporters—the Conservatives advocated more liberal views on voting and other civil policies while the Radicals, including Brownlow, approved of the narrowed political margins.

The Radicals nominated Brownlow for reelection in 1867 and the Conservatives nominated Emerson Etheridge. However, the legislature had given the governor all power over elections, and Brownlow issued a proclamation which would easily assure his reelection. (On February 25, 1867, the Negroes had been given the right to vote, and an act was passed enabling Brownlow to appoint election commissioners for each county who had the power of appointing judges and clerks of elections.) Etheridge withdrew from the race and Brownlow was elected for a second term.

Although the governor had restored order within the state to a large degree, making penalties heavy for even minor crimes, the carpetbaggers and the unstable Negroes still posed problems for the state government and for the general populace as well. Before his second term in office ended, Brownlow' left these problems in the hands of DeWitt Senter and moved to Washington; the governor had been elected to the United States Senate.

Aside from the conflict surrounding the administration,

the state made great strides under his leadership. On July 2, 1866, Tennessee had returned to the Union—the first state to do so. Also during his tenure, the legislature had passed a law providing separate schools for Negroes at state expense. Fisk University for black students had opened at Nashville, the first commercial oil well had gone into operation in Overton County, and the first state agricultural college had been established.

In spite of his iron-fisted rule and the slash of his script in publications, Parson Brownlow is recorded as having been a mild-mannered, docile man in his home, spending his evenings writing by his fireside. He was married to Eliza Ann O'Brien of Carter County, the daughter of James and Susan Everett O'Brien. Her father was a notable iron producer in Carter County. The Brownlows were the parents of seven children.

After his retirement from the Senate, the ex-governor returned to his home in Knoxville and died there on April 29, 1877. He was buried in Gray Cemetery at Knoxville.

Brownlow had been nominated for governor by Unionists in January of 1865 when they had assembled in Nashville to again amend the constitution, and provide for the restoration of civil government. They submitted an amendment abolishing slavery and declaring all acts of the government void after May 6, 1861; and those were the two major changes in the state's laws. But in 1870, under Governor Senter, more revising would occur.

DE WITT CLINTON SENTER
(Whig/Republican)
(1869-1871)

When William Brownlow left his gubernatorial post during his second term to become a United States senator, DeWitt Senter, speaker of the state senate, became governor by succession. He was the second ex-officio high executive. (Hall, following Houston, had been the first.) Senter assumed the office in February of 1869; the official election for governor would not be held until August. In that election, Senter ran for governor against the Radicals' choice, William Stokes. However, as governor, Senter held the same supreme power that Brownlow before him had held and could make the necessary preparations, so in effect the election was already decided. Senter won over Stokes by some 70,000 votes.

Senter's administration inherited the problems not straightened out under Brownlow, as the people of Tennessee tried to work out a postwar pattern for their lives. New concepts must be formed, and old guilts purged. Those involved with the Confederacy were not allowed to participate in any way in government, and carpetbaggers— so termed because they owned no more property than could be carried in a carpet bag—plundered the South, inducing the Negroes, free now and able to vote, into joining a group called the Loyal League. That organization promised great things to the Negroes, provided they voted for the men the league selected. Organized in Tennessee, the Loyal League, like other secret organizations that sprang up after the war, became a disguise for villainy and a terror for the people. Fortunately, it never carried much political weight in the state.

In opposition to the league there arose the Ku Klux Klan, and its popularity swept the country. History has ascribed the group's origination to Pulaski, around 1866, although later reports dispute this statement. Supposedly formed first by a group of Confederate veterans, the Klan was to have been a type of social club where pranks were pulled on individuals—blacks in particular—as the members, in mimicry of dead soldiers, dashed over the countryside wrapped in white sheets and hoods, with their horses swathed in white at times as well. But the Klan became a terrorist group and grew more violent in its methods. Negroes and Negro sympathizers were flogged and tortured. Klan members also sought to bring their own brand of reasoning to wayward husbands and fathers; and in in their efforts at correction committed even greater crimes, leaving the coals of flaming crosses behind them. Anyone could commit crimes under the cloak of white and transfer the ominous deeds to the Klan. Many notorious charges were assigned to them that, in truth, were not all their own. Laws were passed to suppress the organization, and some of its members were sent to the penitentiary.

But the Klan was not the only concern of administration. In the legislature that met in 1869, the Democrats had a majority in both the house and senate, and new laws were in the making. Laws were passed to sustain the credit of the state; investigation was made into the state debt and the railroads to which bonds had been issued; the laws giving extraordinary powers to governors were repealed; and the right to vote was restored to male citizens who had been living in the state for six months.

The most important work of the Senter administration was the provision for a constitutional convention to be held at Nashville in January of 1870. At the beginning of Senter's term as governor, the people had voted for a revision of the fundamental law, which had not seen a major change in nearly four decades (aside from the civil government's temporary changes).

The assembly of 1870 included a past governor, governors-to-be, and leaders of both the southern and northern armies. Convention delegates, aware that they were being watched by Radical leaders in both Tennessee and in Washington, wisely chose a moderate, John C. Brown, to act as chairman. The revisions made by the group allowed the passage of Negro suffrage, though at the same time applying a poll tax prerequisite for voting that would deter most black voters; placed a restriction on the state's power to lend monies, a hindsight conclusion derived from the state's existing indebtedness; limited the governor's control of the militia; changed the schedule and pay of the legislature (lawmakers could receive pay for only seventy-five days of regular session and twenty of a special session, enlarged the judicial body to five members and stipulated that not more than two could reside in any one grand division of the state; made November the date of state elections on even-numbered years; and gave the governor veto power.

Born in McMinn County in 1834, Senter was the son of William Tandy, a Methodist minister, and Nancy White Senter. Having read law on his own, by 1865, Senter had been elected to the state senate, where he represented Grainger, Anderson, Union, Claiborne, and Campbell counties. He became speaker the following term, and hence found himself in the governor's chair "ad interim" in 1869 and was reelected in August of the same year.

Though Senter was a staunch Union man, like other landowners of his day slaves were a part of his chattel. But he supported the federal cause, and was arrested by the Confederates during the war and was their prisoner for six months.

In 1859 Senter had married Harriet T. Senter, a third cousin eleven years his junior. She was the daughter of Colonel P. M. Senter, who had fought in Florida in 1857 and in the Mexican War. Harriet Senter was born in 1841 at Bean Station, the noted location of the first frontier log cabin at the Watauga Settlement. Her mother was Adeline McGraw, a notable Tennessee surveyor.

Harriet was educated at the Rogersville Academy for Women. She favored the domestic life, and enjoyed the quiet environs of home, much as she had enjoyed the farm

DeWitt Clinton Senter
1869-1871

William Gannaway Brownlow
1865-1869

James Davis Porter
1875-1879

John Calvin Brown
1871-1875

days of her youth. She avoided the public eye, remaining with her husband's mother while he was in the executive chair in Nashville. He boarded there while governor, and she visited the capital when occasion presented itself. (There was no governor's mansion there as yet.)

At the close of his administration, Governor Senter retired to his home in Morristown. He died there June 14, 1898, and was buried in Jarnigan Cemetery. Though reared in a strict Methodist atmosphere, he was not affiliated with any church. The Senters had no children.

JOHN CALVIN BROWN
(Whig/Democrat)
(1871-1875)

Giles County spawned John Calvin Brown, the third governor to go out from the county. The two other Giles Countians were "Browns" also, and Neill Brown (1847-49) was John Calvin's brother seventeen years his senior.

In 1827, John C. Brown was born to Duncan and Margaret Smith Brown, who were of Scottish descent. He was educated in the Old Field Schools prevalent in Tennessee at that time, and at Jackson College in Columbia. He studied law with an uncle, Hugh Brown, at Spring Hill, and started his own law practice in Pulaski by the time he was twenty-one; the year was 1848. In a short time, young Brown had secured a lucrative practice in Giles and the surrounding counties. Even though he was a man of pronounced political views, he did not seek a political office, but devoted his zeal to his profession.

The question of secession was upon the lips of all Tennesseans, and Brown was quick to give his opinion favoring the Union, making vigorous speeches in behalf of a united government. But events were happening fast— South Carolina and Mississippi seceded, Fort Sumter was fired upon, Tennessee began organizing troops for the inevitable War Between the States; Brown stood with his fellow Tennesseans and entered the fight.

Enlisting as a private in the Confederate forces—although he declared he was not joining an army but the service of his state—Brown was soon elected to captain. In May of 1861 he became colonel of the Third Regiment of Tennessee Infantry. He was brigade commander at Fort Donelson when he was captured by Union troops and sent to Fort Warren.

In late August of 1862 he was freed in a prisoner exchange, and was promoted soon thereafter to brigadier-general, assigned to duty with General Braxton Bragg. He participated in the Kentucky Campaign of Bragg early in the war.

General Kirby Smith led a subordinate group from Knoxville, through the Cumberland Gap and defeated the federal troops in a heavy engagement at Richmond, Kentucky. This movement reached Lexington, in the center of the state, and threatened Cincinnati.

Brown was attached to the main forces headed by Bragg, which moved on a line west of the Cumberland range toward Louisville, on the Ohio River. A severe action at Perryville, with no definite victory for either side, caused a withdrawal back to central Tennessee.

Later he fought with General Joseph Johnston in battles in the Georgia vicinity, including those of Chickamauga and Mission Ridge. Another promotion put him at the rank of major-general, and he thus served under General John B. Hood in the battles fought on Tennessee soil. Having been wounded in Perryville and Chickamauga, he was again among those to shed his blood at Franklin, on the last day of November in 1864.

When the war was over Brown resumed his law practice in Pulaski. In 1870, he became a member of the Tennessee

Constitutional Convention and served as president of that body while the new constitution of 1870 was written and adopted. The following year he took the governor's chair under the new constitution and was reelected in 1872, the first Democrat to be elected governor of Tennessee after the war. He had been a strong Whig supporter, but, after that party died out, he allied himself with the Democrats.

Many of the state's vexing problems left over from the war had been either solved or passed over by the time John C. Brown took the gubernatorial position in 1871 following Senter's administration. Two major issues which needed his immediate attention were the huge state debt and the frail school system.

The state debt had risen steadily since 1833, when the state issued interest-bearing bonds and used the money from the bonds to establish a bank. Bonds had been issued to purchase the Hermitage, to build the capitol, and to fund numerous other projects. The debt totaled some three million dollars by the time of the Civil War. The state then had lent its credit to turnpike companies, plank road companies, and railroads until a debt of nearly fourteen million dollars had piled up by the time troops tore the state apart. With such companies crushed by war, the state was left with the debt.

By the time Brownlow took the governor's office in 1865 the debt had skyrocketed. Apparently too busy restoring law and order to the state, Brownlow did little to reduce the debt from 1865 to 1869, and even added to it. Thus when Brown became governor in 1871, the debt hung like a weight over the state. During his two terms in office the state's bonded debt was reduced from forty-three million dollars to around twenty million dollars and a floating debt of three million dollars paid.

The public school system was an even greater incubus. Negroes had been made citizens, but they had no education. Desiring to help meet the need of black children as well as white, especially the rural children, Governor Brown went to work on education. By 1873 a school law was passed that provided for a state superintendent of public education, a county superintendent in each county, and city superintendents in the individual cities. A board of three school directors in each school district was to be established, and schools for blacks and whites were to be created separately, in accordance with laws already passed. To pay for this public school system, Brown's administration levied a state tax and authorized counties and cities to levy additional taxes for the same purpose; the first public school system was in progress.

Brown was unseated by James D. Porter in 1875, after which he ran for United States senator but was defeated by ex-president Andrew Johnson. With his political life ended, Brown returned to his home and law practice in Pulaski.

He had two marriages. The first was to Anne Pointer, daughter of John and Martha Pointer of Spring Hill. Anne died in 1858, leaving no children. In 1864, Brown married Elizabeth Childress, originally of Murfreesboro but who was living in Griffin, Georgia, at the time of their marriage. Elizabeth was the daughter of Judge John W. Childress, a major in the Confederate Army, who had sought exile in Georgia when the federals were in Tennessee. At that time, Brown was fighting in Georgia with the Confederates, and there met and married Elizabeth who would become the state's first lady.

In Pulaski, the Browns lived where Martin College now stands. Their four children grew up there, with a portion of their youth spent in Nashville. (Their oldest daughter became the wife of Benton McMillin, who would become governor twenty-eight years after her father.)

In later years, Brown was appointed receiver of the Texas Pacific Railway Company and moved to Texas for a while. He was elected the company's president in 1888; in 1889 he became president of the Tennessee Coal and Iron Company, the largest industrial corporation in the South at that time. In August of 1889, he died at Red Boiling Springs, Macon County, Tennessee. He was buried at Pulaski.

JAMES DAVIS PORTER
(Democrat)
(1875-1879)

The Democrats selected James Davis Porter their candidate for governor in 1875, choosing him to run aganist the Republican choice, Horace Maynard. Porter won the election by well over 40,000 votes. His administration, like that of Carroll's in the 1820s, marked a period of peace and growth in Tennessee. The people had rolled up their sleeves and were at work rebuilding what the war had destroyed. New churches, homes, and businesses were established across the state, as old grudges and hates and differences were put to rest.

James Porter was born in the town of Paris, Tennessee, on December 7, 1828, to Dr. Thomas Kennedy and Geraldine Horten Porter. Of English-Irish descent, both his parents were from well-to-do, educated families. Porter received his early education in the Paris community schools, and at fifteen entered the University of Nashville. He earned his B.S. degree there by age eighteen, and later the degree of LL.D. from the same university. Like other young lawyers of his day, a part of his education in law was study under a proficient older lawyer. And if that lawyer happened to have a pretty young daughter of marrying age, as did wealthy John Dunlap under whom young Porter studied, then that was all the better.

John H. and Marietta Beauchamp Dunlap had moved to Paris from East Tennessee in 1823, settling there about the same time as Dr. Thomas Porter. The two men were friends, and both were civic leaders in West Tennessee. Dunlap owned a great deal of smooth farming land in that part of the state, and left much of it to his daughter Susannah, who became the wife of James Porter in 1851. She had been educated in the Nashville Female Academy, and was a fitting spouse for the personable young lawyer on his way to the governor's chair.

Taking up a law practice in Paris, Porter was soon involved in Tennessee's early political affairs, and was elected to the legislature in 1859. He put politics aside, however, at the outbreak of the Civil War. He first served as General Pillow's adjutant general, and assisting in the organization of troops and then became General Cheatham's chief of staff, remaining in that position until the war ended.

After the war, Porter picked up his legal career again in Paris, remaining in practice from 1865 to 1870, when he was made judge of the circuit court of his district. From this position, he entered that of the governorship in 1874, and his family moved with him to Maxwell House in Nashville.

On the agenda of governmental affairs, the state debt loomed heavy. Like Governor Brown before him, Porter urged the legislature to work hard at removing a part of the weight. The state's creditors had agreed to accept three-fifths, or sixty cents on the dollar, with 6 percent interest, as payment in full on all their claims. This agreement would be labeled the "sixty and six" compromise.

Porter urged the lawmakers to accept it, but the 1876 legislature adjourned without passing a bill in its favor.

In other areas, Porter fought to keep public schools at their best, inefficient as they were at the time; the first Negro Medical College (Meharry) was founded, as a part of Central Tennessee College; a "four-mile" liquor law was passed by the legislature, aimed at prohibiting the sale of liquor within four miles of a school; and the state fought hard to overcome an epidemic of yellow fever.

Following four years in the governor's chair, Porter became the president of the Nashville, Chattanooga, and St. Louis Railroad, a post he held for four years. President Cleveland appointed him secretary of state in 1885, but he gave up that position after two years and became a trustee of the Peabody Educational Fund; he was instrumental in establishing George Peabody College for Teachers in Nashville. Porter served as president of that college for four years, and was a member of Board of Trustees of the University of Nashville, the college where he had received his education.

He also served, at President Cleveland's appointment, as minister to Chile, resigning that office in 1896. When William Jennings Bryan was making his pitch for the presidency, Porter was suggested as his opponent. The ex-governor refused the opportunity, noting, "The *Nashville American* referred to me as a man of sixty years, so I am too old to run for President."[9]

After his retirement, Porter returned to his home in Paris where he died May 18, 1912. He was buried there in Old Dunlap Cemetery. His widow died two years later. They had been the parents of six children, three of whom met early deaths.

[9]Walker, *Out of a Clear Blue Sky*, 185.

ALBERT SMITH MARKS
(Democrat)
(1879-1881)

By 1879, the oaks and poplars that spread themselves across Tennessee's hills were not looked to as protection against the arrow and the musket. The signs of war had passed for most when Albert Marks took the gubernatorial chair, although the new governor's missing foot and leg would be constant reminders of its reality. No longer were the slaves in sight. Now there were no uncles nor aunties nor mammies—but individuals, men and women and children, their "marses" swept away by the strokes of progress.

Marks was born in Daviess County, Kentucky, on October 16, 1836. His parents were of Virginia ancestry. His father, Elisha Marks, died early, leaving the fourteen-year-old Albert manager of a fairly large estate. Such heavy responsibilities interrupted his education, but did not stop it. His parents had designed their son for the ministry, but Albert Smith Marks preferred to enter the study of law. He was a diligent student of jurisprudence, studying on his own much of the time, and was admitted to the bar at Winchester in 1859. He then joined the firm of Colyar, Marks, and Frizzell.

Even though Marks was a Union man, when the Civil War began, he went with the state, entering the Confederate Army. He was elected captain, and soon thereafter rose to colonel of the Seventeenth Tennessee Regiment. In the Battle of Murfreesboro in December, 1862, Marks was severely wounded in the foot while leading a charge, and amputation of the foot and leg was necessary. At the time of the injury, he was engaged to seventeen-year-old Novella Davis, whom he offered to release from her betrothal. She refused exemption however and at nineteen became his wife.

After the amputation of his leg, his health and vigor regained, Marks refused to quit the army. He returned to the field of battle and was made judge advocate on the staff of General Forrest, where he remained until the end of the war. His gallantry at Murfreesboro placed him on the Confederate roll of honor.

During the war years, he married his faithful Novella, the daughter of John B. and Caroline P. Hunter Davis of LaGuardo in Wilson County. Following her husband as closely as battles would allow, Mrs. Marks lived at various places in Mississippi and Georgia while he was with the army. Their first child was born at LaGrange, Georgia.

When the fighting was over, the future governor and his family returned to Winchester, where he resumed his law practice. A second son was born to them at that location. In 1870, Marks was elected chancellor for the Fourth Chancery Division and remained in that position until he was elected governor in 1879. As chancellor, he compiled a remarkable record. Finding the dockets of his division filled with cases that had never been settled, Marks promptly let the lawyers know that such cases must be tried. His warning proved successful; the dockets were cleared, and justice did not have to be delayed.

When Marks became governor, the state debt hung just as heavy over his administration as it had over Porter's and Governor Brown's before him, and he urged the legislature of 1879 to do something about the problem. The sixty and six compromise had been rejected by previous lawmakers; now an act was passed to settle the debt at fifty cents on the dollar with 4 percent interest. The creditors were willing accept this proposal; but when the vote was put before the populace, they rejected the "fifty and four" proposition, and therefore, the state still struggled under the weight of its liabilities.

Partly because of the vexing problem of the debt, Marks did not seek renomination in 1880. He did become a candidate for United States senator, but was defeated by William B. Bate. But his practice of law, which he resumed in Nashville, was enough to keep him busy, and his services were sought after by individuals throughout the state.

Marks died in Nashville on November 4, 1891, and was buried in Winchester Cemetery. His widow died in 1906 at Lebanon, and was buried beside him.

ALVIN HAWKINS
(Republican)
(1881-1883)

Alvin Hawkins was born in Bath County, Kentucky, on December 2, 1821, and came to Tennessee with his parents when he was four years old. His father, John M. Hawkins, of English descent, was a man of the land who had first settled in Maury County and then moved on into Carroll County to "put his roots down proper."

Young Hawkins attended public schools in the area, and then entered Bethel College at the age of eighteen. The future governor taught school for a short while, and, not finding his fulfillment as a pedagogue, entered the study of law. After a year of study with the noted Benjamin Totton, Hawkins was admitted to the bar. He became a partner with a cousin, Isaac Hawkins, and in 1843 opened his own legal practice in Huntingdon, where he remained for ten years prior to his entry into the legislature as a representative from Carroll County.

A strong Whig supporter, Hawkins favored the Union, and fought the state's secession all the way; but to no avail. He joined with the Republicans after the dissolution of the Whig party, and Andrew Johnson—as military governor—appointed him to Congress in 1861. But with the disruption of politics during the Civil War, Hawkins never served as congressman. He returned to his law practice in Huntingdon, and was made United States attorney for West Tennessee in 1864. However, after a year in that position, Hawkins resigned to accept an appointment as judge of the supreme court of the state. He had served on the bench three years when the constitution of 1870 displaced him, and he again took up his law practice.

Elected governor in 1881, Hawkins took the chair at a time when the state debt was paramount in Tennessee's political problems. As Marks and Porter had before him, Governor Hawkins urged the legislature to attend to this burdensome problem.

In April of 1881, the lawmakers passed an act to repay the money dollar for dollar, with 3 percent interest. But the act was not put before the people, and that negligence brought about a split among the taxpayers. A suit was filed to prevent issue of the bonds. The state supreme court decided in favor of the citizens and the plan to repay the debt was rejected.

A second attempt at ending the debt was a proposed graded-interest settlement, repaying sixty cents on the dollar with 3 percent interest for the first two years, 4 percent the next two years, and 5 percent after that time. Even though this proposal looked good to Tennessee lawmakers, the creditors rejected the plan, and the debt of a war-torn state hung heavy over it at the end of Hawkins' administration.

The Republicans nominated Hawkins for a second term in office, while the Democrats ran William Bate. And a new party had sprung up, sure that its members could remedy the troublesome money situation. The Greenback party, as it was called, taking its name from its doctrine that government should issue more treasury notes so as to make money more plentiful, nominated John R. Beasley. Bate defeated both Beasley and the incumbent, and the state debt was passed on for the Democrats to ponder.

During his term as governor, Hawkins' son, Ernest, had served as his secretary in Nashville. The governor and his son resided at the Maxwell House Hotel in that city, while Mrs. Hawkins and the other five children remained at the family home in Huntingdon. Mrs. Hawkins was the former Justina Ott of Murfreesboro.

History records the governor as a large, forceful individual, fond of his family and homelife, and his lay position in the Methodist Church.

After a long political life he died from pneumonia at his Huntingdon home on April 27, 1905. He was eighty-four. Mrs. Hawkins had died four years earlier. They were buried in the family cemetery at Huntingdon.

WILLIAM BRIMAGE BATE
(Democrat)
(1883-1887)

William Bate inherited the state's financial millstone when he took office in 1883. The Democrats had wrested the governor's chair from Hawkins after one term by more than 27,000 votes, sure that they could find a way to settle the problem of Tennessee's indebtedness.

Bate was born to James and Amanda Weathered Bate in Sumner County in 1826, and was reared at Bledsoe Lick, now called Castalian Springs. His father died when William was fifteen, which threw the responsibility of running a farm on Bate's teenage shoulders. He received his early education in one of the academy schools of that period—a one- or two-room building, built of logs, with grade levels running into the junior high level.

By the time he reached twenty-one, Bate had finished
his academic studies; but like many of his contemporaries
who would prove themselves leaders of men in the political
realm, he must first show his strength in the militia. He
thus enlisted in the Mexican War, and was among the first
Tennesseans to reach enemy country. After proving his
prowess as a fighter, he returned to Castalian Springs to
become the editor of a Democratic newspaper there before
entering politics as a state legislator.

Bate was graduated from Lebanon Law School when
he was around twenty-six years of age. He opened a law
office in Gallatin in 1852, and in 1854 he was elected
attorney-general of the Nashville District.

By 1861, when the rumble of war crossed the South,
he joined the Confederate Army, becoming captain and
then colonel of the Second Infantry, which was noted for
its stamina during the Civil War. The brigade fought with
the army of North Virginia during 1861 and 1862, and was
associated with General Albert Johnson south of the Tennessee River. In the Battle of Shiloh, three members of the
Bate's family were killed—a brother, a brother-in-law, and
a cousin—and he was severely wounded in the leg. The
doctors urged amputation, but Bate would not hear of it.
He survived the injury, kept the leg, recuperated for
awhile, and then, returned—on crutches—to the fight; he
was promoted to brigadier-general by Jefferson Davis,
president of the Confederate government.

At the close of the war, Bate returned to the family
farm at Castalian Springs. He opened a law office in
Nashville and was soon one of the best-known lawyers in
the area. By 1883, he had become governor of the state,
and inherited the state debt trauma.

The Democrats, fearing that the Republicans would
continue at the helm of politics in 1882, and quick to
blame them for the state's burden anyway, had united

William Brimage Bate
1883-1887

Albert Smith Marks
1879-1881

Robert Love Taylor
1887-1891, 1897-1899

Alvin Hawkins
1881-1883

behind Bate as leader of the state, and in 1883 had supported his proposals all the way in settling the debt. They
agreed to pay parts of the bonds against the state in full—
those held by Mrs. James K. Polk, and some to educational
and charitable institutions. Those to the railroad companies
were paid at fifty cents on the dollar and 3 percent interest;
the balance of the debt was divided into three parts—some
of it paid at seventy-six cents, some at seventy-nine cents,
and some at eighty cents. The weary creditors accepted the
offer, and the debt that had plagued Tennessee for over
fourteen years was put to rest. No doubt the Democrats
were quick to claim this accomplishment as their own.

With the debt question settled, Bate was naturally
elected for a second term, which went well for him and the
state as a whole, for it could look now toward growth and
peace.

While governor, Bate and his family lived on Russell
Street in East Nashville. He had married Julia Peete,
daughter of Colonel Samuel and Susan Pope Peete of
Huntsville, Alabama, in January of 1856. When Julia was
three years of age, her mother had died, and she was reared
by an aunt in a true antebellum atmosphere at Huntsville.
Samuel Peete, a graduate of William and Mary College, had
moved to Huntsville from Sussex County, Virginia, in
1819 and had become an influential attorney. Julia Peete
Bate bore the governor four daughters, two of whom died
young.

Following his years as governor, Bate was elected to
the United States Senate where he remained until the time
of his death. He died in Washington on March 9, 1905, five
days after sitting on the cold platform in front of the
United States Capitol, where he had watched the second
inauguration of Teddy Roosevelt. His body was returned
to Nashville for burial in Mount Olivet Cemetery.

ROBERT LOVE TAYLOR
(Democrat)
(1887-1891; 1897-1899)

Perhaps the most talked about gubernatorial campaign in the state was that of Robert Love Taylor. Tennesseans had long loved an evening of fine speeches from the stump and now, in the Taylor campaign, a touch of ironic humor had been added to a bit of familial sting handled in great style, as Robert L. ran against his own brother.

Robert Taylor was born in Carter County on July 31, 1850. His parents were Nathaniel Green and Emaline Haynes Taylor. Educated at Pennington, New Jersey, and at Athens, Tennessee, young Taylor had begun a law practice in 1878. Having entered politics that same year, he was elected to Congress as a Democrat, even though he was from a Republican district. He had given a part of his time as editor of the *Johnson City Comet,* and having shown his skill as an orator during the presidential election of 1884, Robert became the Democrats' candidate for governor in 1886, the same election in which his brother Alfred would run on the Republican ticket.

The Taylor family was close-knit, and Tennesseans knew that nothing really bad would come out of their contest. When someone made the statement that "they were two roses of the same garden, though different in their political views," [10] the populace was quick to pick up the theme of the famous War of the Roses between the royal Yorks and Lancasters. The Democrats donned the white rose of York in support of Bob, and the Republicans took the red rose of Lancaster as they backed up Alf. Women arranged their color schemes accordingly in their dress and their boudoirs (if they could afford to), and the men's politics were revealed by the rose in their boutonnieres.

[10] Wilma Dykeman, *Tennessee: A Bicentennial History* (New York: W. W. Norton and Company, 1975), 112.

politics were revealed by the rose in their boutonnieres. Never had the crowds been better entertained in a political rally than during the Taylor brothers' campaign.

Charismatic, warm, and congenial, they were both fiddle players, serenading one another with string and anecdote.[11] Or they spoke with grave dignity on issues that required their solemn attention, such as the United States Navy, where events were moving fast. Tennessean Matthew Maury had made a great splash for himself shortly before in his work with the navy, establishing the national observatory, and directing endeavors that led to the development of ocean cables and telegraphs and signal services.

When the votes were counted, Bob had won over his brother, and Alf good-naturedly stepped aside. The most noted event during Governor Taylor's administration was the repeal in 1887 of a state prohibition measure which the legislature had passed two years earlier. In other areas, the Taylor administration promoted laws to enforce honest elections. One, the Dortch Law, specified that in the more populated areas, voters should mark printed ballots in secrecy unless blind or handicapped; and another, the Lea Election Law, was designed to avoid federal interference in state elections, and still another law confirmed the payment of poll tax as a prerequisite for voting, as required by the constitution of 1870.

Taylor was known as a "pardoning governor." Censured for his philanthropic endeavors by evangelist Sam Jones for having pardoned so many prisoners, Taylor answered, "If it hadn't been for the pardoning power of

[11] Folmsbee related in *Tennessee: A Short History* that some people claimed Nathaniel Taylor wrote the speeches for both his sons; and that on one occasion Bob delivered Alf's speech after the two had reached the platform, leaving the embarrassed Alf to construct another—impromptu.

God Almighty, you, Sam Jones, would have been in hell long ago."[12]

Taylor was married three times. First, he wed Sarah Baird, who died after giving birth to five children (who lived in the home of "Alf" and Jennie Taylor). Bob then married Alice Hill of Tuscaloosa, Alabama, and that marriage apparently ended in divorce. In 1904, he married Mamie L. St. John, daughter of a Virginia lawyer.

After a four-year term, and later a two-year term as governor, Taylor traveled and lectured; he then served in the U.S. Senate from 1907 to 1912. He died in Washington on March 31, 1912. His body was returned by train to Knoxville, where he was buried in Monte Vista Cemetery at Johnson City.

JOHN PRICE BUCHANAN
(Farm-Labor)
(1891-1893)

Buchanan was the first farmer to be elected to the office, though other governors had owned farms and derived a part of their livelihoods from the soil. During the Bate and Taylor administrations, unrest had developed among the agriculturists of the state. They issued a cry which echoes yet across the land—that the government's policies were oriented more toward the professional and commercially-minded individuals than toward the farmer. In an attempt to make their voices heard, the protesters formed farm groups for political strength. First known as the Grangers and the Wheels, these groups evolved into the stronger Farmers' Alliance which took an active part in the politics of 1890. The results of their efforts climaxed in the election of John P. Buchanan for governor.

[12]Walker, *Out of a Clear Blue Sky*, 213.

Buchanan was a man of the soil, bound close to the earth, and the common men felt sure that he would be thus bound to the problems of the farmer. However, they were disappointed; prison riots and an insurrection of coal miners that had grown out of a change in the prison lease system took the governor's primary attention. The prison lease system had been a controversial issue for a number of years.

Because of the cost of operation of the penitentiary (recorded at $15,000 a year), the legislature wanted a law that would ease this heavy burden for the taxpayer. An act had been passed to appoint a board of directors for the institution which would hire out the convicts to the highest bidder; thus the prisoners would be forced to work instead of receiving support at public expense. They were therefore hired out for less than one dollar per day per prisoner. In protest of these punitive measures, the convicts burned the shops of the firm where they were first hired. The firm not only refused to pay for their labor, but demanded restitution for damages, which the state paid.

With over 1,000 men confined to punishment at that time, the penitentiary became a money-making business. The arrangement created disturbances among coal miners of the period, for employers now preferred the cheap prison labor, throwing the regular miners out of work. The end result was a revolt of the miners in 1892.

In a concentrated effort to terminate this threat against their livelihoods, the miners attacked the prisons at Tracy, Briceville, Oliver Springs, and Inman, releasing the prisoners and burning the buildings. Governor Buchanan sent in troops to restore order, but the men were poorly trained and even less equipped for fighting. Finally, the riots were brought under control by the National Guard, composed of Tennessee's First, Second, and Third Regiments, after numerous lives and much property were destroyed.

Possibly Buchanan's greatest contributions were the enactment of a secondary school law which included the study of Tennessee history and civics in the high school curricula and the granting of Confederate pensions.

John P. Buchanan was the son of Thomas and Margaret Sample Buchanan. He was born in Williamson County on October 4, 1847; his ancestors were friends and associates of James Robertson and with Robertson pioneered the settlement of Nashville in 1779 and founded Buchanan Station in 1782.

Buchanan received a common school education, and at sixteen joined the Confederate Army, serving in Alabama under General Nathan Bedford Forrest. Four years after the war, he married Frances McGill, the daughter of James and Amanda Norman McGill of Rutherford County. Frances had attended the country schools of Rutherford County, and then a girl's school at Woodbury, Tennessee.

Buchanan became a prosperous farmer, and his voice was heard among farm groups that were experiencing trying times. He was elected to the legislature in 1886 and again in 1888, and became president of the Farmers' Alliance which dominated the state Democratic convention in 1890. Buchanan was nominated to run for governor against three other candidates—Josiah Patterson of Memphis, father of future governor Malcolm R. Patterson, John M. Taylor of West Tennessee, and Jere Baxter of Nashville.

While her husband was busy with politics, and after he took over the gubernatorial chair, Mrs. Buchanan remained on the farm with their children, visiting the governor in Nashville when she saw a fitting opportunity. A Rachel Jackson type, she managed the stock, the planting, the harvesting, and her eight children.

Certain that he would be defeated on the Democratic ticket for governor in 1893, Buchanan was persuaded to run for a second term on an Independent party ticket. He did, and lost.

He parted with politics and returned to his farm, remaining there until 1926. In that year, the Buchanans moved from their farm to Murfreesboro, where Mrs. Buchanan died November 30, 1927. The ex-governor died May 14, 1930, and was buried in Murfreesboro. He was Presbyterian.

PETER TURNEY
(Democrat)
(1893-1897)

Buchanan lost his second bid for the governorship to the Democratic candidate, Judge Peter Turney. Turney too had first made his mark in the militia, serving with the Confederate Army as colonel of "Turney's First Tennessee Regiment." He was severely wounded at Fredericksburg, declined a promotion because he didn't want to leave his men, and returned with the regiment to Winchester after the surrender of the Southern forces. He was elected judge of the supreme court of Tennessee in 1870, 1878, and 1886; and from that latter year until he became governor, he remained the chief justice of the state.

Turney was born in Marion County in 1827, the son of Hopkins L. and Teresa Frances Turney. Hopkins Turney was a United States senator, selected by the "immortal thirteen." The governor's mother was the daughter of Hannah Henry and Miller Frances.

Educated at Winchester and Nashville, Turney studied law under his father and by 1848 had gone into his own practice. A forensic and determined secessionist, he is recorded as having already organized a regiment and

Peter Turney
1893-1897

John Price Buchanan
1891-1893

James Beriah Frazier
1903-1905

Benton McMillin
1899-1903

started on his way to Virginia when Governor Harris issued the proclamation that Tennessee's tie with the United States was dissolved. The group had left Tennessee in great spirits, his soldiers cheering madly, as they rushed toward the bloody fight. But in the fray Turney received a slug that entered his mouth and lodged in his throat—too near the jugular vein for removal, so the army physicians decided—and he was sent home to his family.

After recuperating, he returned to the war, this time to command troops in Salt Lake City, Florida. His wife and children followed him to reside in Monticello, Florida. And their home in Tennessee, which was being looked after by their slaves, was burned by federal troops.

Turney's First Tennessee Regiment surrendered at Appomattox; less than a hundred of his men returned to Tennessee soil. After his discharge, the bullet in Turney's throat was safely removed by qualified surgeons.

Turney took up his law practice once more and returned to his civic affairs and a lay position in the Episcopalian church. In 1870, he was elected judge of the supreme court and remained in that position until he became governor.

His administration saw the end of the prison riots and the penitentiary lease system, absolved by the purchase of a large tract of land near Cumberland River northwest of Nashville, where Brushy Mountain Prison was erected. Coal deposits in the acreage, mined by the prisoners, furnished fuel for the capitol, the asylums, and many other public buildings. That ended the state's vexing matter of prison riots, but in 1894, it had another problem—two governors.

Turney was a candidate for reelection in 1894; the Republicans ran Clay Evans of Chattanooga, who at first seemed to have won the contest. But Turney claimed that some of those who voted had not paid their poll taxes, and he insisted he was entitled to the office that Evans had

taken over. After investigation, the legislative body discovered many voters had not paid for their right to vote.
Since the counties containing the most fraudulent votes
were cast for Evans, Turney was declared the governor and
Evans was removed from the governor's office, for which
he had already taken an oath.

But the most exciting time of Turney's four years in
office was the celebration of the state's Centennial. Talk
had begun when Turney first took office of this festive
celebration which would be held June 1, 1896. A committee was appointed in 1894 and land south of Nashville was
purchased for the exhibit. It was to be a grand affair,
exhibiting the best of Tennessee's arts, inventions, industries, and products from the land. People were enlisted
from all over the United States to engage in the activities.
But to the committee's chagrin, they were not ready for
the opening of the event and the state's birthday had to be
postponed until it was one hundred and one years old; in
May, 1897, the Tennessee Centennial Exposition became a
reality, and it remained open until the fall.

Governor Turney, already near retirement age at his
election, and who had already served as supreme court
judge for twenty-three years, lost his bid for a third term
to Robert L. Taylor, who had filled the executive chair
already from 1887 to 1891.

Turney had two marriages, the first to Casandra
Garner, the fifteen-year-old daughter of Thomas and
Elizabeth Wadlington Garner of Franklin County, whom
he married in June of 1851. Mrs. Turney died six years
later, leaving three children. He then married Hannah
Graham, whose parents were John and Aletha Roberts
Graham of Davidson County. Nine children were born to
this union.

After leaving the governor's chair, Turney resumed his
law practice in Winchester, but poor health prevented his

active service in the courts. He died in 1903 and was buried at Winchester.

BENTON McMILLIN
(Democrat)
(1899-1903)

Among McMillin's voluminous contributions to Tennessee history is his famous—or infamous—Income Tax Bill.

Benton McMillin was born on September 11, 1845, in Monroe County, Kentucky, the son of John and Elizabeth Black McMillin. Educated in Kentucky schools, first at the grade-school level and then Kentucky University, he moved into Tennessee where he studied law with Judge E. L. Gardenshire in Carthage. In 1871 he opened his first law practice in Celina and built up a thriving practice. By 1879 McMillin had made his way to the United States Congress where he was reelected continuously until 1898, serving over twenty years in that body before becoming governor the following year. He was a member of the Committee on Ways and Means for fourteen years, and the Committee on Rules to the end of his term of service.

McMillin first married Marie Childress Brown, daughter of the early governor John C. Brown (1871-75) and Betty Childress Brown of Pulaski. They had one son, and Mrs. McMillin died soon after his birth. She was buried at Pulaski. McMillin then married Lucille Foster in 1888, and they had one daughter. Her father, James Foster, was a wealthy cotton planter in Louisiana, and her mother was one of the first suffragettes in the South.

The Feminist leaders of the 1970s would be envious indeed should they examine the record of this Tennessee first lady, who made her mark in history just at the turn of the twentieth century. Lucille Foster McMillin would have taken a back seat to none where women's rights are concerned. Nancy W. Walker records her as gallantly riding mule-back through the jungles of Peru, where no woman had gone before, while her husband served as minister to Peru for seven years after he left the governor's chair. Returning to America, Lucille lectured extensively on women's suffrage and women's place in the world. She was state president of Tennessee Federation of Women's Clubs, the first national committeewoman and the regional director of Democratic Women of Southern States. In this capacity, she worked among eleven states. Lecturing at universities, she also gave alumni and baccalaureate addresses, and was the recipient of an honorary degree from the Lincoln Memorial University at Harrogate.

Aside from those activities, Mrs. McMillin was appointed to the highest office held—that far in history—by a woman. Franklin D. Roosevelt appointed her as Civil Service commissioner in 1933. She remained in that position until 1946 when ill health forced her to retire. But this book is concerned with the lives of the governors, not their wives . . . .

For more than a century, some degree of ill will had existed between Virginia and Tennessee in regard to the line dividing the two states. The argument went back to the period when Tennessee was a part of North Carolina. There had been confusion about the dividing line then, but the two states compromised on a boundary, and surveyors marked the line. However, the prints had faded with the passage of time, and in 1859 the two states appointed a joint committee to remark the line. But the line was not confirmed by the legislature of both states; thus in 1889 Virginia requested the Supreme Court of the United States to establish the old charter lines as the true boundary, rather than the compromise line. The court refused, setting the boundary lines in the latter compromise agreement as correct, neither did the court have the line permanently marked. Therefore, in 1901, McMillin took it upon his administration to see that the dividing line between the two states became a definite entity, and requested the state supreme court to appoint a committee to permanently mark the boundary, thus ending the age-old dispute.

McMillin's Democrat-controlled legislature turned their whole attention to state improvement. Solid educational laws were enacted, including a law which empowered school boards in each county to establish a high school; and a tax, not to exceed fifteen cents on each hundred dollars of taxable property, was passed to support such establishments. Other school laws provided for the election of school directors for each school district; uniform textbooks throughout the state were adopted, along with the agreement from publishers that the material content not be changed for five years after adoption, and appropriations were made for teachers' institutes.

Financially, Tennessee had a good four years under McMillin. Reforms were made in the judiciary system which increased the annual state revenue by some $30,000. A tax was levied on all corporations, bringing in some $40,000. The new penitentiary system, inaugurated in the Turney administration, furnished another $100,000, bringing the state a rather stationary income.

McMillin was not a candidate for a third term. The Democrats therefore ran James B. Frazier, who was elected. And it would be under Frazier's administration that the Democrats would adopt a platform to finally approve the troublesome prohibition measure.

After leaving the governor's chair, McMillin went into an insurance business in Nashville, and died in that city on January 8, 1933. He was buried in Mount Olivet Cemetery, where his widow, who had lived in Washington since his death, was buried beside him in 1946.

JAMES BERIAH FRAZIER
(Democrat)
(1903-1905)

James Frazier was among the last of those blue-blooded statesmen who traveled about erect and proud in coaches with gas lanterns at each side, pulled by roans and sorrels, soon to be usurped by the era of motors and fast moving wheels. Frazier was born in Bledsoe County in 1857, the son of Judge Thomas N. Frazier, for many years judge of the criminal court in Davidson County, and Rebecca Julien Frazier.

Educated at the University of Tennessee where he was graduated by age twenty-one, Frazier married Louise Keith in 1884. She was the daughter of Alexander Hume and Sara Foree Keith. Her father was a successful attorney and a wealthy planter. Her grandfather, who came to Tennessee from Virginia in 1820, was judge of the circuit court in Athens, Tennessee.

Loquacious and chivalrous, young Frazier set up a law practice in Chattanooga following his marriage, and soon gained recognition. His speeches, plus his vigor and fair-mindedness marked him for a leader in the state, and by 1903 he was elected governor. His family moved from Chattanooga to the Tulane Hotel in Nashville, which was home for them while he remained in the executive chair.

Governor Frazier's administration is described as one of wise management and a prosperous period for the state. Seeking to improve the public school system, barely an infant in its progress, Frazier asked the legislature to pass the Romine Bill, which would allow any unappropriated monies in the state treasury at the beginning of each

January to be added to the public school fund. From each source, Frazier proffered to the state treasury $271,600 in his first January following (1904).

He appointed Seymour A. Mynders as state superintendent of public instruction, and this appointment marked the beginning of an era in education in the state. Mynders was the first professionally trained and experienced educator in that position, and he brought a zeal to education heretofore unequalled, organizing the schools into a strong political force.

At the time of Mynders' appointment, Tennessee law prescribed only six months of school, and even that requirement was not enforced in many counties. There were 6,758 schools with grades ranging from one through five, 1,069 going from one through eight, but there were no high schools. Of the state's 771,965 students only 484,663 were enrolled in places of learning, and only 341,538 in regular attendance. That meant less than 50 percent of those eligible were attending schools. The average monthly pay for teachers was $28.86. The lowest paid teachers were those in Van Buren County, who received $18.50 per month, and the highest were in Shelby County where pay was $40.72. However, will must have been the major requisite for teaching, for teacher training was hard to come by in those days. No state colleges for teacher training had been built in the state by 1900, but George Peabody College for Teachers appropriated state funds to be used for scholarships and for the support of teachers' institutes.

In 1903, Mynders brought school administrators together in Nashville to propose a strong platform for educational improvement and to launch a campaign to achieve these objectives. The platform called for an increased state school fund, local taxation to support education, school consolidation, better training for teachers, establishment of libraries, establishment of at least one high school in each county, elimination of politics and nepotism from the schools, and intelligent and economical expenditure of school funds. Out of this campaign for education would come the General Education Law of 1909, and that bill would lead to the enactment of a measure in which education was to receive 25 percent of the annual gross revenue of the state, to be distributed among counties. Hence, education was on its way as a major institution, pulling its own weight as a lobbyist in the political realm. Where the troublesome prohibition measure was concerned, the Democrats at last adopted a measure which prohibited the sale of liquor in towns of 5,000 inhabitants or less, which would leave barely a half-dozen cities across the state wet.

In other legislation, a law was passed regulating state mining and providing inspections of mines to prevent unsafe working conditions. Heavily enforced, this law prevented explosions in mines, and accidents were lessened. Rioting and trouble among miners was not yet ended, however, and Frazier, like Buchanan, faced riots at Coal Creek. He went directly to the men, and through persuasion brought the problems to an end. Frazier also improved agriculture and manufacturing, and the commercial interests in the state.

He resigned the governorship in 1905 to take the seat of United States Senator William B. Bate who had died on March 9. (John Isaac Cox, speaker of the state senate, filled out Frazier's unexpired term.)

Senator Frazier moved his family to Washington where he served in the Senate until 1921.

He died in 1937, and was buried in Forest Hill Cemetery at Chattanooga.

JOHN ISAAC COX
(Democrat)
(1905-1907)

While James Frazier was serving his second term as governor, United States Senator William Bate (former governor) died in Washington. Frazier was elected to fill the vacancy and left the Tennessee governorship, the third to resign that office. John Isaac Cox was then speaker of the state senate and thus succeeded Frazier to the governor's chair ex officio, in accordance with the constitution. He was inaugurated governor on March 27, 1905, after having entered the senate in 1900.

Cox was born in Sullivan County on November 23, 1857. His father, Henry W. Cox, who was killed in the Civil War while fighting with the Confederates, was of a family that had been among the pioneers of Tennessee. There were eleven Cox brothers who came from England to settle with the Jamestown settlers. Four of the brothers moved on into Tennessee, and were signers of the Watauga Compact, the first written constitution of the western world.

Cox grew up in poverty. His widowed mother hired him at age ten to a farmer for twenty-five cents a week. Thus with poverty at his heels, he made his own opportunities. By age sixteen he had been given the position of rural mail carrier, and by eighteen he was appointed road commissioner. He had studied at the Old Field Schools in Sullivan County, and determinedly worked his way through Blountville Academy. Becoming a student of law next, he studied with Judge W. V. Deaderick and is recorded as having married the judge's daughter. But if so (nothing further was found on this marriage), he also married Lorena Butler, daughter of Dr. Matthew and Mary Dulaney Butler of Blountville by 1905. She was the cousin of Bob

and Alf Taylor (governors of Tennessee). Her great-grandfather was Andrew Taylor, who was among the Watauga
settlers. An educated young woman for her day, Lorena
Cox had studied in Sullins and Maryville colleges, and in
Cleveland, Tennessee. A son and a daughter were born to
her and the governor.

Opening his own law practice in Blountville, where he
soon became the county judge and then the county attorney, was his stepping-stone to success. By 1889 he had
moved on into Bristol and become the city attorney, and a
year later was elected senator. The year 1905 found him in
the speaker's chair, and from that position he rose to that
of governor following the resignation of Governor Frazier.

As governor he was efficient, and careful of the state's
affairs, handling his role in a businesslike manner. Serious
rioting at Tracy City and Whitwell had to be repressed, and
was; quarantine laws for keeping yellow fever out of the
state were enforced; a state flag was adopted, designed by
LeRoy Reeves; and the old soldiers' pensions were increased, ironically enough, by the man whose mother was
left in poverty by the desolation of war. Pensions were
approved for either Confederate or federal soldiers or their
widows, so long as the recipients drew no other aid from
the United States treasury. The state also bought 11,000
acres of land in Bledsoe, White, and Van Buren counties to
be used as a place for convict labor. Cox was known as
anti-prohibitionist, and his influence helped defeat the
application of prohibition to more cities during the 1905
legislative term. His reign has been labeled by historians as
a period of "thrifty activity," a term which seems a trifle
obsolete in the present era, when superfluous red-tape and
paperwork expense casts equally long red shadows on the
government's balance sheets.

The governor lost his bid for a second term in 1907,
defeated by Malcolm R. Patterson. However, in the same

year, he was elected to the state senate. He served in that body until 1911.

Following his retirement, Cox lived in Bristol where he died on September 5, 1946. He was buried in Sullivan County, near Bristol. Mrs. Cox died in 1951.

MALCOLM R. PATTERSON
(Democrat)
(1907-1911)

Tennessee had been a state for 110 years when Malcolm Patterson became its chief executive. But in the entire century, no place had been built to house the governor and his family while he was in office. In 1907 the legislature, with Governor Patterson's approval, appropriated money to purchase a building in Nashville to be used as a governor's mansion, and the building next to it to be used as extra office space for handling state affairs.

Such a move on the part of the lawmakers stirred public opinion no end. Some of the citizens complained that rented homes or hotels in the city would serve just fine for the first families, since governors had been using them for over a hundred years. But progress being what it is, a fund was set up to buy a home for the family of the state; and the Patterson family was the first to occupy it.

Malcolm Patterson was born in Summerville, Alabama, on June 7, 1861. His father, Colonel Josiah Patterson, commanded the Fifth Alabama Cavalry in the Confederate Army during the Civil War, and his great-grandfather, an army man as well, was Alexander Patterson, a leader in the Revolutionary War. Of Scotch-Irish descent, and a pioneer in Abbeville, South Carolina, the elder Patterson migrated on into northern Alabama and married Mary Deloache, daughter of John Deloache, who owned a large farm where the stone and steel structures of Birmingham now stand.

Malcolm R. Patterson
1907-1911

John Isaac Cox
1905-1907

Ben Walter Hooper
1911-1915

Thomas C. Rye
1915-1919

Moving farther north, Josiah settled in Florence, where he practiced law, having purchased the now historical Pope's Tavern there, today the Florence City Museum. He is recorded as having lived in the building five years, before moving his family on to Memphis, where he again set up a law office.

Malcolm Patterson attended the Memphis area schools, receiving his higher education at Christian Brothers College and at Vanderbilt University. After studying law in his father's office, Malcolm opened his own office and by 1884 had been made attorney general of the criminal court at Memphis, a position he held for six years. He was sent to Congress in 1900 as a representative of the Tenth District. After three years in Congress, he became governor in 1907, unseating Governor Cox.

While he was governor, Patterson married Mary Russell Gardner, daughter of William and Jenny Sutherland Gardner of Obion County. He was the third Tennessee governor to marry while in office. Patterson was several years his wife's senior, he having had two previous marriages. His first wife was Lucille Coe Johnson, daughter of Malcolm and Sara Coe Johnson of Memphis; three children were born to their union. Patterson then married Sybil Hodges of Philadelphia, and one daughter was born to them. His third wife, Mary Russell, helped rear the children of his former marriages and gave him two additional children—a daughter, born in the mansion, and a son, born after the governor left office.

Patterson's administration was a progressive one for the state, partly because some of the projects reaching fruition during his term had their beginning before he took office. Too, culture was rapidly changing—the automobile was coming to the land, and cities must be joined by asphalt; thus a State Highway Commission was established. The prohibition controversy, begun earlier, was taken up

anew by the Women's Christian Temperance Union and
the Anti-Saloon League in their efforts to change the old
adage that Tennesseans spent more money for booze than
for bread. The General Assembly of 1909 passed a bill
prohibiting the sale of intoxicating liquors anywhere in the
state within four miles of a school. Governor Patterson
vetoed the bill, raising the eyebrows of his followers, for
he had pledged to support prohibition in his canvass for
governor. He maintained that his support was promised
under specific conditions, the conditions being that the
people should want such a law and that they be given the
opportunity to express themselves freely regarding it,
either pro or con. To support his veto, he insisted that
people had not been given such opportunities, while the
legislature informed him that they were elected with in-
structions from the voters to pass such a bill. So they over-
rode the governor's veto, making prohibition a state law.

Although Patterson and his legislature could not agree
as to prohibition, they did see eye to eye on education,
and were credited with some of the best moves in public
education, including the passage of a County Board Law
for public schools.

The Patterson administration cleared the western part
of the state of the Night Riders, who had taken up a private quarrel with a land developing firm regarding development of a tract around Reelfoot Lake. Feeling that the
firm was trying to beat them out of their property and
fishing privileges, a group of West Tennesseans had formed
this secret terrorist organization. The Night Riders took it
upon themselves to rid the country of one of the land
firm's lawyers by hanging and shooting him. Their antics
brought fear to the innocent, and the governor, campaigning for his second term in office when the terror
arose, put his plans aside and headed for Obion County.

Here he called out the state guard and soon had the matter under hand in short order.

The voters liked such gallant actions on the part of the governor, and voted him a second term; but this term brought their reprimands. In action similar to that of Bob Taylor before him, Patterson pardoned 1,412 criminals, and he was sharply criticized for his action. Law officers rebelled at the thought of catching criminals only to have the governor turn them loose. He was accused of being more interested in "machine politics" than in trying to enforce laws. Friends of Patterson disagreed, upholding the governor's actions. The split in opinion divided the Democratic party in Tennessee into two camps—the Independent Democrats who opposed him, and the Regulars who supported him.

Political excitement again became intense in the state, and partisan feeling bitter. The Regulars appointed a man for each office to be filled at the following election, including that of governor, judges, supreme court justices, and other offices; and the Independents did likewise.

The Republicans endorsed all the Independents in the upcoming August election, and the Independents were elected. Patterson ran for a third term, supported by the Regular Democrats. But the Republicans had nominated Ben Hooper for governor, and the Independent Democrats went with him. Patterson withdrew from the race with the dilatory conclusion that he did not want to cause division in the Democratic party.

After leaving the governor's mansion, the Pattersons moved again to Memphis and built a home there where they lived until the ex-governor died in 1935. He was buried in Forest Hill Cemetery at Memphis. Mrs. Patterson lived until 1956. They were Presbyterians.

BEN WALTER HOOPER
(Republican)
(1911-1915)

Prohibition was still the nucleus of the political strife when Ben Hooper took the oath as governor in 1911. Hooper, the Republicans' choice, had also been endorsed by those of the "Independent Democrats" because of a split in the regular Democratic party the year before.

Chaos in regard to liquor sales and the liquor law ran rampant in the state; prohibition had been passed in 1909, but the flow of liquor had not been halted. As a legislator, Hooper had introduced the Four Mile Law for small, incorporated towns which prohibited the sale of liquor within four miles of any rural school. But the law was not passed statewide until 1909 under Patterson.

Hooper was a religious individual who was not afraid to let his light shine from the podium, and made prayer a very large part of his canvass for governor. The frustrated populace felt sure that here, at last, was a man who would enforce the prohibition law, and internal strife in the state would cease. But as it turned out, Hooper's administration was one of the most turbulent in the state's history.

In his inaugural address, Hooper had pledged his support to a clean and businesslike administration. He had been elected by both Republicans and Democrats, and his yoke was heavy; he had to please all. He selected both Democrats and Republicans for those offices normally filled at the governor's appointment. In 1911, he sent his proposals to the legislature for the good of the state; but with the tension between the Regular and Independent (Fusionist) Democrats over prohibition and election laws of 1909, passage of any bill was hardly probable.

The Fusionists, who consisted of both Independent Democrats and Republicans, had a majority in the house while the Regular Democrats controlled the state senate, and there was dispute galore. Fusionists fled the halls of government to prevent the formation of quorums, and before the legislative business was finished, armed guards were called in to keep them at their places long enough to take care of the state's affairs. Ed Crump, the powerful political voice, who permitted open saloons in Memphis as an expedient to power, worked on the Fusionists' side during the first part of the session but switched to the Regulars after Hooper called for enforcement legislation designed to close the saloons in Memphis.

In spite of this turmoil, however, Hooper's administration authorized counties to issue bonds to buy school property and to establish hospitals. A child labor law was passed. A law stipulating that working women's pay should be issued to them only and a Pure Food and Drug Act was passed.

Hooper was elected for a second term, defeating former governor Benton McMillin, and the legislature of 1913 proved even more uproarious than in 1911. Dispute over prohibition and election laws ran rampant; some of the meetings were little more than street riots, with both Democrats and Republicans filibustering at will to prevent the passage of measures.

Nevertheless, some legislation was enacted. Hooper's second term saw a law passed increasing state revenue for education and a compulsory school law requiring children between eight and fourteen to attend school at least four months out of the year. County boards of education were authorized to transport pupils to and from school; official examination of state banks and banking systems was provided for; the parole system for convicts was investigated; and the method of execution for the death penalty was changed from hanging to electrocution. Sanitation laws were passed and improvements planned for farming areas.

After much pressure from the governor, the legislature passed the "Jug Bill" and the "Nuisance Bill." The former prohibited the shipment of intoxicating liquor to and from places within the state and the delivery of more than one gallon of liquor to any one person by shipment from areas outside the state. The "Nuisance Bill" provided that ten citizens of any community, where policemen or other officials would not act, might go before the courts to secure the closing of bawdy houses, saloons and gambling houses.

Ben Walter Hooper's life bore a resemblance to those of the first pioneer leaders, who were goaded by ambition. He was born at Newport, Tennessee, on October 13, 1870. Orphaned in his early years, he spent his childhood in the St. John Orphanage of the Episcopal Church at Knoxville, receiving his education there and at Carson Newman College.

He studied law in the office of Judge H. N. Cate, and then opened his own practice. In 1893 and 1895, he served in the legislature, that first rung past law school on the politician's climb. But he took time from his ascent to enter the Spanish-American War, where he was captain of Company C, Sixth United States Volunteer Infantry. After the war, he was elected as the assistant district attorney for the Eastern District of Tennessee, his final stride toward the governor's chair in 1911.

In 1901 he had married Anna Bell Jones, a wealthy young woman of high status. Her parents were Benjamin and Townsella Randolf Jones of Newport; her father was the first merchant in Newport. Governor Hooper's was the second family to occupy the state mansion. A son, their fifth child, was born to them there, and later a sixth child was born.

After leaving the governor's office, Hooper joined the Railroad Labor Board in Chicago for awhile, but he re-

mained active in the Democratic party and was elected
vice-chairman of a limited constitutional convention in
1953. He died at Carson Springs in 1957, and was buried
at Newport.

THOMAS C. RYE
(Democrat)
(1915-1919)

The state looked to Thomas C. Rye to steer it from
1915 to 1919. Rye had received the reputation of a stern
attorney general in Paris, Tennessee, from 1910 to 1914,
where he had shown an unbending attitude toward boot-
leggers. He was equally firm in enforcing the law in all
other areas, and insofar as the populace was concerned,
this alone was enough to receive the vote of the common
man when the Democrats ran the relatively unknown
Henry County attorney as their candidate for governor in
1914. The state had been plagued enough with unlawful
liquor dealing, and Rye, a prohibitionist and unattached to
party factionalism, was acceptable to party leaders
throughout the state. He was supported by Luke Lea,
founder of the *Tennessean*, and by former governor
Patterson who, once on the fence where prohibition was
concerned, had turned teetotaler and was supporting now
the American Anti-Saloon League, lecturing throughout
the state in support of law and order—and of Rye for governor. Rye won the vote by 137,656 to 116,667.

In spite of the unending political strife in Tennessee,
during Rye's administration the state's growth flourished,
mainly because of that paradox of war which brings pros-
perity to the materially minded and horror to the human-
ist. World War I had begun. An aluminum plant (Alcoa)
had come to Maryville, offering employment to hundreds.
A munitions factory was established at Hadley's Bend,

near Nashville, offering more employment. And in 1917, when the United States declared war against Germany and President Wilson appealed to the states to prepare for the conflict, Tennessee—in traditional fashion—responded dramatically, with 80,000 Tennesseans entering the fight.

Possibly the most notable contribution of Rye's term was his promotion of the Ouster Law, whereby any office-holder could be ousted from his post if he proved incompetent, and those places filled in turn by more proficient individuals. This bill was aimed at eliminating Memphis Mayor E. H. Crump, rising political boss in West Tennessee who refused to close the city's saloons. Suit was filed against him in 1915, and he was ousted from office as mayor, but his voice would not be quieted in the state for some thirty years thereafter, when Estes Kefauver would refute his influence in the Senate election of 1948.

Other legislative measures under Rye included the creation of a State Highway Department; founding of a central board, appointed by the governor, to have control over the state's penal and charitable institutions; organization of a State Board of Education to have nine members, three of them to be of the minority party, with the governor appointing three members from each of the state's divisions, designating one as chairman; and levy of a state high school tax of five cents on each $100 of taxable property, the money to be used in the county where it was collected.

Thomas Rye was born in 1863 in a log cabin in Camden, the son of Wayne and Elizabeth Atchison Rye. He grew up on his father's farm, attending public schools in Benton County. But by the time he turned twenty-one, he had successfully completed a study of law in Charlotte, North Carolina, and by 1884 had returned to set up his own law practice in Camden.

In 1888 he married Betty Arnold, daughter of Aaron and Josephine Arnold. They moved to Paris where Rye became district attorney general in 1910, an office which he resigned to accept the highest state office in 1915.

At the close of his four successful years as governor, Rye returned again to law practice in Paris, where he was active in civic and church affairs (Cumberland Presbyterian).

He died on September 12, 1953, and was buried at Paris. Mrs. Rye died in Nashville in 1961. They were the parents of two children.

ALBERT H. ROBERTS
(Democrat)
(1919-1921)

Albert Houston Roberts was born in Overton County on July 4, 1868, the son of John and Sarah Carlook Roberts. He received his early education in the area schools in Overton County, and attended high school in Kansas where his family moved when he was an adolescent. Following his graduation, he returned to Tennessee and entered Hiwassee College in Madisonville, from which he was graduated in 1889. In the same year, he married Nora Dean Bowden, whose father was an instructor in Latin at the Hiwassee College. Miss Bowden had also been a student at the college.

After their marriage, Albert and Nora lived in Madisonville where Roberts was a teacher at Alpine Private School for five years. His wife taught music in the same school. Roberts was then appointed county superintendent of public instruction and served two terms before entering upon the study of law and opening his own law practice. He remained involved in legal offices for fifteen years, and was made chancellor of the Fourth Division of Tennessee, the position that he held when he was elected governor.

In 1919 he took over the governor's chair, defeating his Republican opponent, Judge H. B. Lindsey, with a canvass that hinged upon Roberts' promise to the people of the state that he would provide a conservative and businesslike administration. The day following his inauguration, he delivered a strong address to the general public. Drawing upon the policies of Governor Carroll almost a hundred years before him, Roberts charged Tennesseans to put the good of the public above individual, selfish desires; to live within their incomes, and to avoid debt; and he promised the same for the state's operation.

A number of important events marked the Roberts administration, including a revision of the tax laws of the state, removal of the inequalities of assessment and providing fair measures of evaluation on property, especially those concerning large business enterprises; the levying of a direct school tax to be equalized in schools over the entire state; passage of the State Police Bill, supposed to prevent lynching and mob violence; and a workmen's compensation law, whereby an employee or his family could automatically receive payment for damages resulting from his injury without a lawsuit. Women were granted the right to vote for municipal offices and for president and vicepresident of the United States; the state ratified the Eighteenth Amendment (prohibition) to the United States Constitution; the battleship *Tennessee* was launched and christened in Brooklyn Navy Yard; and a State Memorial Building was erected in Nashville.

The erection of the latter evolved as a result of the celebrated Alvin C. York's welcome back into the country following his heroism in World War I. And it seems fitting enough that Tennessee, which had 2,000 soldiers for the War of 1812 under Governor Willie Blount, and for Governor Aaron Brown 30,000 offspring of Revolutionary patriots, many of whom would become quiet shadows at Shiloh, should yield as well an even nobler twentieth-century son.

When the United States declared war on Germany in 1917, York, a peace-loving Fentress Countian, felt the same tug within that had stirred his forefathers to the battlefronts. He immediately entered the U.S. Army and was shipped out to France, and there Sergeant York became the most famous enlisted man of the war. Surely the earth covering the graves of John Sevier and Campbell must have echoed reverberations of "Come on boys, let's get 'em" that eventful October day in 1918, when in the Argonne Forest, commanding a squad of only seven men, York killed twenty-five Germans, silenced thirty-six machine guns, and took one hundred and thirty-two prisoners, including four officers.

For this extraordinary service, the French awarded Alvin York their highest honor, the Croix de Guerre, and his own government bestowed upon him the Congressional Metal of Honor. The legislature of Tennessee gave him a gold medal of honor and the rank of colonel for life. Friends presented him a farm and a home; and Governor Roberts and the first lady provided for Alvin C. York and his bride a wedding in the governor's mansion, the first wedding to be held therein. And because Tennessee could not now lose its image as the Volunteer State, the legislature authorized the erection of a State Memorial Building in Nashville to commemorate the deeds of the state's valiant soldiers.

At the close of his administration Governor Roberts and his family took up residence in Nashville, and still later moved to a farm near Nashville where he died on June 25, 1946. (Mrs. Roberts had died in 1932.) Roberts was buried in Good Hope Cemetery at Livingston. He and his wife were Methodists, and the parents of four children.

ALFRED A. TAYLOR
(Republican)
(1921-1923)

In 1908, the Democrats had started electing the gubernatorial candidates by a statewide primary rather than selecting them in convention, and in the August primary of 1920 Governor Roberts was their candidate for a second term. But the Republicans ran Alfred A. Taylor again. Though older now than when he had campaigned against his Democratic brother Bob, Alfred Taylor still had a winning way at the podium, with his humor and wit and the support of his family, who provided string music and singing to back up his speeches. Apparently, Tennesseans had grown weary of the Democrat mania and turned to Harding in the presidential election and Taylor in the gubernatorial race. The oldest governor to occupy the executive chair, Taylor won his place by more than 40,000 votes.

Alfred A. Taylor was born on August 6, 1848, in Happy Valley, East Tennessee. His parents were Nathaniel Green and Emaline Haynes Taylor. The governor's ancestor, Andrew Taylor, had come with the settlers from Rockbridge County, Virginia, into the Watauga Valley, afterward to be known as Happy Valley.

Nathaniel Taylor was a graduate of Princeton, a politician in his own right, and evidently led his sons in the paths of democratic principles, since one went the way of the Democrats (Robert L.) and one chose the Republican road. In 1864, the elder Taylor moved his family to New Jersey where he was to serve as commissioner of Indian affairs under President Andrew Johnson. There the older children studied, and upon returning to East Tennessee, entered Wesleyan University at Athens.

Alfred, a student of law, was admitted to the bar in 1870. He was elected to Congress in 1875, serving one term; elected again in 1889, he served in the congressional body until 1895.

At age thirty-four, he married fifteen-year-old Jennie Anderson, whose father was a well-to-do farmer and the owner of fine horses in Carter Valley. They were to have ten children. After four years of marriage, Alfred was the unsuccessful candidate for governor against his brother Bob. But later, after many years in Congress and other political involvements, Alfred Taylor became governor. He had lived almost three-quarters of a century when he was inaugurated on January 15, 1921.

The state had just ratified the Nineteenth Amendment (women's suffrage) to the United States Constitution when Taylor took the governor's chair. Women had been previously granted the right to a limited vote—but they held out for full rights to the polls. Now, much controversy stirred the land. Conservative politicians, preachers, and other citizens felt that ratification of the amendment would cause women to lose their femininity, and that such drastic measures might result in war of the sexes.

In spite of the suffrage controversy and Taylor's problems with a Democratic legislature, his administration was beneficial to the state. Laws were passed creating the office of state tax commissioner, expanding the power of the Railroad and Public Utilities Commission, providing money for the establishment of Andrew Johnson's tailor shop in Greeneville as a shrine, creating the Tennessee Historical Committee to collect and preserve antiquities of the state, providing a Mother's Pension Fund Act, and providing for equalization of property assessments for taxation.

Taylor's major contribution may have been his involvement with the nitrate manufacturing plant in Muscle

Albert H. Roberts
1919-1921

Alfred A. Taylor
1921-1923

Austin Peay
1923-1927

Henry H. Horton
1927-1933

Shoals, Alabama. The government spent millions of dollars during World War I in the erection of Wilson Dam, one of the units of Muscle Shoals, which was to have been the site of a huge nitrate plant used in the manufacture of munitions for the war. The Armistice was signed, however, before the project was completed, and the government was about to abandon the site. Governor Taylor, like others who were alarmed at this threat toward progress for the Tennessee Valley area, headed a delegation to Washington to persuade Congress not to abandon the Muscle Shoals project, but to convert the facility to the development of water power to light the valley, and the nitrate plant to the production of fertilizers for the farmers of the South.

He was able, too, possibly because of the venerability of his age, to restore quiet to labor disturbances that arose in sections of the state between expanding unions and the state's growing industries.

In spite of Taylor's age, he ran for a second term in office, but was defeated by Austin Peay.

Following his retirement from office, Taylor enjoyed his large family and the fellowship of his many friends. He died on November 24, 1931; Mrs. Taylor died in 1934. They were buried in Monte Vista Cemetery at Johnson City.

AUSTIN PEAY
(Republican)
(1923-1927)

Austin Peay went down in history as the "Road Building Governor." He found most of Tennessee's roads in mud, as had his predecessors, but he left more than 6,000 miles of hard-surfaced highways behind him. The legislature of 1923 created a Department of Highways and Public Works, and competent road construction began under the supervision of a single commissioner who displaced three

in the course of the reorganization program which Peay
was to head.

Under Governor Peay, 7,500 miles of surfaced highways were completed in nine years; with the advent of the
automotive age, gasoline tax plus the automobile-license
tax would prove a source of revenue for such innovations.
Tennesseans proposed to float a $75 million bond issue for
highways, pushing progress along as much as possible. But
the governor feared such enthusiasm, recalling the state's
past debt trauma, and opposed the plan, encouraging instead a pay-as-you-go policy.

Peay's platform pledge, following that of Robert
Taylor's second administration, was to administer trust
and justice to all people within the state, regardless of class
distinction. Throughout his campaign, he had maintained
that he would "rather be right than be governor." Such
strong appeals for truth and justice in government won the
approval of the Volunteers, and in the November election
he dissuaded many Republicans from supporting Alfred
Taylor, from whom Peay won the governor's seat by
141,002 to 102,586 votes.

Peay was sworn in on January 16, 1923, in Nashville's
Ryman Auditorium, with one of the greatest turnouts ever
to attend a Tennessee inauguration. His friends and supporters had urged a major change in state government, insisting that too many extravagances and too much waste
were taking their tax money. In their presence, Peay
pledged big, and publicly prayed for strength to support
his promises; his administration has been recognized as one
of the half-dozen truly outstanding ones in Tennessee.

Peay's legislature was primarily Democratic, and supported his views. The affairs of government took on new
perspectives under the "Reorganization Bill" that went
into effect in February, 1923. This bill aimed to secure
better service and to promote economy and efficiency in

government; under it, Peay reorganized the sixty-four departments of government—that employed more than 1,000 workers—into eight departments with a commissioner to head each one. In his first appeal to the legislature (January 16), Peay urged the passage of the reorganization measure. Two weeks later the bill, entitled "An Act to recognize the administration of the state in order to secure better service and thorough coordination and consolidation, and to promote economy and efficiency in the work of the government . . ."[13] was enacted. It went directly into effect, reducing the aforementioned departments to the following eight: finance and taxation; agriculture; highways and public works; education; institutions; health; insurance and banking; and labor. Some of the existing agencies were abolished, but most were consolidated. This law was Peay's great contribution to state government.

True to his word, the governor selected men from all sections of the state to head the reduced departments. He understood the farmer and his needs, and reduced his land taxes. The ownership rights of Reelfoot Lake—disputed for years—were worked out under Peay, and the hunting and fishing privileges there were put under the control of the state game warden. A national park was established in the Great Smoky Mountains in 1926, the boundaries to be determined by the Southern Appalachian Park Commission. The state furnished 231,000 acres of Tennessee soil to the project, to which Peay gave a great deal of his time.

Under his administration, education was strengthened, with emphasis on rural school development. In 1925, the state provided funds, by levying a tobacco tax, to enable every rural school to have a minimum term of eight months, and also a schedule was established whereby the

[13] McGee, *A History of Tennessee*, 303.

teachers of the different counties drew a uniform salary for the same grade of work.

The 1927 legislature provided funds to be prorated at the two-to-one ratio (the state giving two dollars to the county's one dollar) for building and repairing county schools. In advanced areas, education was extended in agriculture, home economics, and teachers colleges.

Also occurring during Peay's term was passage of the Anti-Evolution Bill which forbade teachers in any public school "to teach any theory that denies the story of the Divine Creation of man and to teach instead that man has descended from a lower order of animals." But like Missourians, Tennesseans want things proved, so some of them decided to set up their own test case. In Dayton, a small Tennessee town, where methodical individuals started their day at sunup and ended it at sundown, a young teacher, a lawyer, and the owner of the drug store, were discussing the new statute. After examining a copy of *Civic Biology*, which the teacher, John Scopes, had been using as a text—both to stir up some excitement for the sleepy town, and to test the new Tennessee law—the drug store owner stepped to the telephone and called the *Chattanooga News*, informing the press that they had just arrested a man in their town for teaching evolution.

Soon the whole country was stirred by the report of the fellow arrested at Dayton for teaching evolution in the classroom. There was an eight-day trial and three lawyers to plead the case of the young teacher who had the right to "be free, to think his own thoughts, and to believe as his conscience dictated, not as someone else in the state dictated."[14]

William Jennings Bryan, three-time loser in the race for the presidency of the United States and a champion of the

14John T. Scopes and James Presley, *Center of the Storm: Memoirs of John T. Scopes* (New York: Holt, Rinehart and Winston, 1967), 60.

religious cause, represented the state and Clarence Darrow the defense. (Bryan, after a masterful address on the last day of the trial, became ill suddenly and died a few days later.)

Scopes was found guilty, fined $100, and the law remained on the books until 1967 (although Scopes' conviction was reversed on technical grounds by the state supreme court).

Dayton found itself on the map. Hotels and rooming houses were running over with the curious for weeks afterwards, and tourists made it their business to see that the little Tennessee "monkey town" was on their list of sights-to-see for years. Journalists, playwrights, novelists, and historians—both in America and Europe—are still writing of the event. But no report of the tale is complete without the account of a tourist who stopped in Dayton to ask a native, "Are there any monkeys around here?" "No," the Tennessean replied thoughtfully, "but a lot of them pass through."[15]

Peay, with his keen insight, was able to bring order out of chaos to the state. He put it upon sound footing. The people liked his style, and voted him their governor for a third term.

Born in Christian County, Kentucky, on June 1, 1876, he was the son of Austin, Sr., and Cornelia Leavell Peay. The Peays were well-to-do farmers, and young Austin worked the land and studied intermittently at Washington and Lee College, and at Center College in Danville. After completing a study in law, he crossed over into Clarksville, Tennessee, which lay just over the Kentucky-Tennessee state line, and in 1896 started a law practice.

In 1895, he married Sallie Hurst, daughter of John and Amaryllis Smith Hurst of Clarksville. They were to have two children.

15Dykeman, *Tennessee: A Bicentennial History,* 179.

Remaining conscientious in his role as a lawyer, Peay did not invade the political realm until 1910, when he was elected to the legislature representing Montgomery County. Then, starting as governor in 1923, he led the state through two successful terms. However, by the beginning of his third term, he had developed a heart condition and died on October 2, 1927, the first governor to die while in office. He was buried in Greenwood Cemetery at Clarksville.

HENRY H. HORTON
(Democrat)
(1927-1933)

When Governor Peay died suddenly in October, 1927, Henry H. Horton of Marshall County was speaker of the state senate, and thus succeeded to the governor's chair. Horton was the fourth Tennessee senator to fill out a governor's term—Hall, Senter and Cox having filled similar positions—but he was the first to receive the chair because death had caused a vacancy.

Governor Horton was born in Jackson County, Alabama, on February 17, 1886, the son of H. H. Horton, a Baptist minister, and Lizzie Moore Horton, a descendant of the Irish poet, Thomas Moore. Henry Horton was one of twelve children, an even half-dozen of each sex. He spent his boyhood on the family farm, attending public schools in his area, and at eighteen entered Scotts Academy at Scottsboro. He later attended Winchester College at Winchester, Tennessee, where he was graduated in 1888.

Believing that the West held more opportunities than his own part of the world, Horton went to Hillsboro, Texas, where he taught in the public school system for one year. The year following, he returned to Tennessee to teach at Winchester College, his alma mater, for five years.

However, not finding satisfaction in his teacher's role, he changed his profession to law and was admitted to the bar in 1894.

Two years later, he married Adeline Wilhoite, daughter of John Benton and Elizabeth Bullock Wilhoite, descendants of landed North Carolinians who had settled in Tennessee. A quaint hamlet there bore the family name Wilhoite, derived from a dam and mill built by the Wilhoite family. The Hortons had one son.

Horton practiced law in Chattanooga and in 1907 was elected to the lower house of the legislature. In 1911 he became a resident of Marshall County, spending much of his time on his farm on Duck River, twelve miles from Lewisburg. In 1926, he was elected senator from Marshall and Lincoln counties, and having been elected speaker, thus succeeded to the governor's chair in 1927.

Horton made it plain when he took the chair that he would do all within his power to continue the programs of his predecessor, and he made known the fact that he would seek the office again on his own, following his ad-interim term. And in that direction possibly, Horton promised great things, including the proposition that the farmer's state land tax be removed. That promise alone, plus his determination and apparent honesty, won for him the governor's chair by some 71,000 votes on election day (the largest majority given to a Tennessee gubernatorial candidate).

But before his terms were over, the honesty which the electorate had so admired would be doubted, and Horton would be charged with impeachment for the mishandling of state funds. The state lost some $7 million in 1929 when the financial disaster hung heavy over the land, and banks closed at the onset of the Great Depression. The governor had become involved with the strong political newspaperman Luke Lea and with Rogers Caldwell, a successful businessman who had a number of things going for him, including the ownership of a Kentucky rock asphalt company that was supplying asphalt for Tennessee highways. The two had bought up a number of banks, called the Lea-Caldwell banks. When these banks were forced to close, the state of Tennessee had on deposit there better than $6 million. When Tennesseans learned of this, resentment arose against Lea, Caldwell, and the governor, and when the legislature convened in 1931, wide-spread charges for impeachment were made against Horton. A legislative committee was appointed to draft the articles of impeachment. They charged Horton with conspiracy, together with Lea and Caldwell, to defraud the state. However, the movement to impeach Horton failed in the legislature.

In spite of the controversy, Horton's years in office brought to Tennesseans the abolition of state land tax (but a tax was added on cigarettes), creation of a patrol board and a division of aeronautics, increased support for education (especially that in agriculture), and development of a secondary road system for counties, which would connect lateral roads with the main highways across the state.

In the Peay and Horton administrations, the legislature provided for twenty toll bridges. In 1927 an issue of $11 million in bonds had been authorized to aid in the project, and the bridges were built to connect Middle and West Tennessee at Savannah, Perryville, and near Johnsonville.

Under Horton, the General Assembly made appropriations for placing two of Tennessee's most famous sons in the nation's hall of statues at Washington. And who but the immortal enemies—Andrew Jackson and John Sevier—would they choose to stand in stone, championing forever the fighting spirit of Tennessee.

Even though the impeachment charges had been cleared by the end of Horton's term in office, he did not seek reelection in 1932, as the state struggled with the weight of the Great Depression.

After leaving office, the ex-governor again lived on his farm, and died at his home on July 2, 1934. He was buried in Lone Oak Cemetery at Lewisburg. Henry Horton State Park near Nashville bears his name.

HILL McALISTER
(Democrat)
(1933-1937

Following two of his ancestors into the governor's chair, Hill McAlister took the high office at a critical time in the history of the state. Around $80 million in debt hung over the state yet, and the depression years stretched both behind and ahead of him. But McAlister was confident of his abilities as the state's leading figure, and had based his campaign on the fact that he was from a long line of governors and knew what was best for the people. Before him had gone his great-great-grandfather, Willie Blount (1809-15) and his great-grandfather, Aaron V. Brown (1845-47); then there had been his great-great-uncle, William Blount (territorial governor). So Hill McAlister convinced the populace, on his third try, that he could handle the job, and apparently lived up to his promises.

The son of William King and Laura Dortch McAlister, Hill McAlister was born in Nashville on July 15, 1875. His mother was the great-granddaughter of Lucinda Baker and Willie Blount, and the granddaughter of Sarah Burrus and Aaron Brown.

A graduate of the Vanderbilt University Law School, McAlister hung out his law shingle in Nashville the summer of 1899, and by 1901 he had been appointed assistant city attorney; and after four years of apprenticeship as an assistant, he was returned to that office by popular vote. By 1911 he was elected to the state senate, becoming a Democratic leader in the legislature.

McAlister's proposals began to show up in the legislative measures sponsored that year, including one requiring parents to educate their children and one limiting hours of labor for women and children who were employed in shops and factories.

McAlister called for an investigation that led to the improvement of the Pure Food and Drug Inspection Department founded under Patterson's administration and introduced a bill establishing the Davidson County tuberculosis hospital. He returned to law practice at the end of his legislative service, and in 1919 was elected state treasurer, where he served eight years. Making his first bid for governor in 1926, he lost the race to incumbent governor Austin Peay who died only a few months after his new term commenced and was followed in office by Henry Horton. McAlister tried again in 1928, but lost the second time.

McAlister remained undaunted in his effort to try his hand at helping the state out of its predicament. He had foreseen a financial crisis that seemed inevitable for the country and had warned about it in his two futile campaigns for the governorship. But in 1930, when almost $7 million of state money was lost in banks that failed, the people remembered McAlister's warnings. By then the treasury was empty and state government was at a standstill; in 1931, the General Assembly unanimously called him as treasurer. In 1932 he won the Democratic nomination for governor, wresting the place from three other men, including former governor Malcolm Patterson.

McAlister defeated Republican nominee John E. McCall of Memphis in the November general election, and took the governor's chair the following year, during the worst of the depression. Even so, he launched a sharp-cutting economy program, suggesting to the legislature that the governmental expense be pared by a cool $7 million a year.

Running for the office again in 1934, McAlister stood on his record and advocated still further expense cuts, and won that election. He trimmed the upkeep on the executive mansion for $35,000 to an unbelievable $1,000, insisting that it was unfair of him to request a cut in his employees' salaries and not propose a reduction for himself.

When McAlister announced his try for a second term, more than 25,000 applications for jobs in state services had been received. Instead of hiring more civil servants, however, he reduced them by 2,380 positions during his first term. For months after he took office, McAlister is recorded as having been swamped by officeseekers, and frequently ate his lunch behind his desk, where he usually remained until 7:00 P.M. in the evenings. Often carrying work home with him to ponder over in his study, he gave up his evenings with his family, or sports events which he loved. He was an avid supporter of his alma mater's (Vanderbilt's) football team.

In his speeches, McAlister resorted to none of his predecessors' rabble-rousing; he sounded serious notes and avoided the political custom of joke-telling.

In addition to its economic reforms, the McAlister administration was noted for its support of the Tennessee Valley Authority, opposition to any modification of Tennessee's dry laws, advancement of interest in agriculture, and what the governor called a "friendly attitude" toward labor. McAlister earned the reputation of granting numerous pardons to prisoners, and advocated a policy that would continue to be honest and just, beyond which, he insisted, he could promise nothing further.

Among other activities on the state's roster during the McAlister administration, the iris was adopted as the state flower and the mockingbird as the state bird; the Tennessee State Planning Committee was started; construction on Pickwick Landing Dam began; and industrialists began construction of modern airports in Nashville, Chattanooga, and Memphis, while in the same year, paradoxically perhaps, the "Rebel," Tennessee's first streamlined train, made its initial trip across West Tennessee. Norris Dam was completed, and produced the first power; the state repealed the convict-lease law; and an unemployment compensation law was enacted.

At the close of his four years in office, McAlister and his family moved again to their Nashville home. He had married Louise Jackson in November, 1901, and their wedding was one of the highlights of the fall social season. They were to have two daughters. Louise Jackson was the daughter of Justice Howell E. Jackson of the United States Supreme Court, and Mary Harding Jackson. She had revived the open house custom at the executive mansion, and actively assisted the governor in his campaigns.

Following his tenure as governor, McAlister was appointed field counsel of the Bituminous Coal Commission in Washington, where he served for more than two years prior to being named referee in bankruptcy in January, 1940. He was chairman of the board of elders in the Christian church, and remained an active figure in the Democratic party as long as possible.

Mrs. McAlister having preceded him in death by four years, the former governor died on October 30, 1959, at age 84, and was buried in Mt. Olivet Cemetery in Nashville.

GORDON BROWNING
(Democrat)
(1937-1939; 1949-1953)

McAlister did not seek reelection in 1937. He had run into conflict with Ed Crump, the undisputed political boss of Tennessee, who disagreed with him on many issues, including the liquor question. The Eighteenth Amendment had been repealed in 1931, but with McAlister's support coming from dry counties, he refused to give in to Crump's demands that Memphis and other large cities be allowed to sell alcoholic beverages.

Gordon Browning of Huntingdon was in step with Crump in 1936 and received his support at the poll—and thus the governor's chair in 1937—in opposition to Burgin E. Dossett of Campbell County.

Browning was born in 1895, the youngest child of James and Malissia Brock Browning of Carroll County. The family moved to Gibson County, where his father was justice of the peace. The future governor was christened as Gordon Weaver Browning, but early rejected his middle name. He graduated from Milan High School in 1908, and afterwards taught school and farmed in Gibson County. At the age of twenty, he entered Valparaiso University in Indiana, where he waited on tables to pay his board. He graduated in 1913 with the Bachelor of Science and the Bachelor of Pedagogy degrees, and then earned a law degree from Cumberland University in 1915, entering the practice of law in Huntingdon the same year.

At the outbreak of World War I, Browning enlisted in the National Guard. He fought in France, receiving the rank of captain and a citation for gallantry.

With the close of the war, he reopened his law practice, and in 1920 married Ida Leach, daughter of William and Madonna Baird Leach of Huntingdon. In the same year,

Gordon Browning
1937-1939
1949-1953

Hill McAlister
1933-1937

Jim Nance McCord
1945-1949

Prentice Cooper
1939-1945

Browning was nominated by the Democrats for a place in the United States Congress, but lost the race to Republican nominee Lon Scott. Browning and Scott had been friends at law school, and their friendship continued throughout the campaign, in spite of political differences. They canvassed the Seventh District in joint debate, riding in the same car to save expenses. Scott won the coveted congressional seat, but Browning bided his time and wrested the place for himself two years later, and served in the Congress for six straight terms. Browning was an outspoken representative, championing the rights of the Veteran's Administration and opposing Franklin D. Roosevelt in his attempt to rebuild the nation's economy following the depression years.

In 1937, Browning had been elected to the governor's chair, with Crump behind him. However, friendships and values have the prerogative of change, and in the years following Browning's election, the men became bitter enemies. The highlight of Browning's political career came in 1948 when he combined forces with Estes Kefauver to break Crump's control of Democratic politics in the state.

Browning's administration favored larger appropriations for education, a merit system for state employees, a license for automobile operators, better roads, continued development of TVA, a reorganization of state government, a balanced budget, and refunding of the state debt.

Drawing upon Austin Peay's successful reorganization program, Browning's plan provided, among other things, for a department of administration and an office of back tax collector. He proposed increased taxes on public utilities and chain stores, a corporation excise tax, an increase on the income tax of securities, an increase in the tax on beer and on the franchise tax.

Browning was unseated by Prentice Cooper (who now had Crump's backing) in the following election, but was reelected in 1949 and served two more terms. He did not renew the fierce controversy with Crump, but concentrated on a rural roads program and improvement of educational facilities. In 1951, a law was passed removing the payment of a poll tax as a prerequisite for voting. Browning lost his seat in 1952, however, after being charged with fraud and mismanagement in connection with the state purchase of the Memorial Apartment Hotel in Nashville. He was defeated in the Democratic primary by Frank G. Clement of Dickson.

Even so, Browning did not lose his influence as a political leader, and still had a strong following when he died at age 86. Leaving no descendants, he died on May 23, 1976, and was buried in Oak Cemetery at Huntingdon.

PRENTICE COOPER
(Democrat)
(1939-1945)

Prentice Cooper was a bachelor governor. His mother served as first lady during his six-year stay in the mansion, and those six years were years of transition for the state.

Barely had Tennessee begun to pull out from under the weight of depression when, at the turn of the next decade, it was again preparing for war. During Cooper's terms in office, World War II was fought and won. Rallying again to the call of battle, the Volunteer State furnished 315,501 Tennesseans to help with the task.

By the 1940s, the terrestrial echo of thundering hooves had given way to the spatial drum of planes, and a new and terrible weapon—the atomic bomb—was in the making. Uranium for the bomb, which would first be dropped on Hiroshima, Japan, taking thousands of lives and speeding the war's end, was being produced in Oak Ridge. But atomic operations there were one of the best-kept secrets of

World War II. Even the inhabitants in the area, with the exception of a few men, knew nothing of what was happening in the new city that appeared so suddenly eighteen miles west of Knoxville. The site had been acquired in 1942 by the national government, and by mid-1943 a group of large industrial plants had been built, plus housing which would provide for a city of 75,000 inhabitants.

Other defense plants also sprang up over the state, including a plant in Millington to furnish powder for the Allies; an aircraft plant at Nashville, turning out planes for the British; and a shell-loading plant at Milan. War contracts awarded to Tennessee firms approximated $1250 billion; and various industries producing clothing, arms, and food for the fighting forces employed more than 200,000 men and women.

John Sevier would have indeed been pleased had he been able to glimpse the census report five years after Hooper left the governor's chair. In 1940, there had been 2,915,841 people in Tennessee; by 1950 the population had grown to 3,291,718. Events in the state were moving swiftly, too numerous to record in this brief accounting of the governors' lives. Army maneuvers had begun across Tennessee soil; Camp Peay at Tullahoma was renamed Camp Forrest in honor of General Nathan Bedford Forrest; and Camp Campbell was opened near Clarksville, named in honor of Governor William Campbell.

Evidently a "seer" where governmental affairs were concerned, Cooper in 1940 appointed a Tennessee State Defense Council, which was the first such council in America. (This was four months before the proclamation of a national emergency and a year and a half before the declaration of war against Germany, Italy, and Japan).

Born September 28, 1895, in Bedford County near Shelbyville, Prentice Cooper was the son of W. F. and Argie Shefner Cooper. He was educated in Bedford area schools, and in Webb Preparatory School at Belt Buckle. He first entered higher study at Vanderbilt University, but transferred to Princeton, graduating in 1917 with a B.A. degree. Following his graduation, he enlisted in the army for service in World War I and trained as an officer, but the Armistice was signed before he became actively engaged in service.

In 1921 he received the LL.B. degree from Harvard University, and went into law practice in Shelbyville the following year, opening his own office next door to that of his father, a noted lawyer and banker.

The voters sent Cooper to represent them in the Tennessee House in 1923, where he served only one term. But in 1925, he was elected district attorney general of the Eighth Judicial Circuit, and city attorney of Shelbyville.

Cooper remained in law until 1936 when he was elected to the state senate, and thence to the governor's chair three years later. It became his task to guide the state through its mobilization from a time of peace to a time of war, and the state took a major step in issuing a million-dollar national defense bond to purchase Sewart Air Force Base in Smyrna.

But matters within the state needed attention, too, and of major significance to the state's well-being was the home-food-supply program created by the governor to improve the nation's health standards. His legislature passed the first civil service act for state employees, and passed a "local-option" liquor bill over Cooper's veto.

The amount of state debt was reduced under Cooper from $123,598,000 to $83,517,000—the largest amount of debt reduction ever accomplished in the state's history. Aid to schools was increased by 66 percent, although World War II made havoc of the public schools as both students and teachers left education for employment in defense plants; and old age assistance was doubled. Free textbooks were provided for children in lower grades, a statewide system of tuberculosis hospitals was inaugurated, and more lands were added to parks and forests.

Governor Cooper had been the first governor since Harris to serve the state three consecutive terms. After leaving the executive office, he was appointed ambassador to Peru, and his mother went along with him to serve as an ambassadress. Cooper served in that position from 1946 to 1948.

In 1950 the former governor married Hortense Powell, daughter of Ferdinand and Margaret McGavock Hayes Powell of Johnson City. They were to have three sons.

Cooper took up his law practice in Shelbyville following his service in Peru, and in 1953 he was elected to the constitutional convention that would add new dimensions to the state laws. Both he and Mrs. Cooper retained an interest in the state's historical organizations, and in civic and church (Lutheran) affairs.

Prentice Cooper fell victim to cancer in his late sixties, and died on May 18, 1969, at Mayo Clinic in Rochester, Minnesota. He was buried at Shelbyville.

JIM NANCE McCORD
(Democrat)
(1945-1949)

Jim McCord was another of Tennessee's colorful governors. History records him as a "self-made man," a "plain-country Democrat," and as "pure and wholesome"—traits that were again taking on significant values for Tennesseans following the jarring influence of World War II. After the clamor for gasoline-ration books and food stamps, and endless hours of waiting in lines for cigarettes and candy bars and ladies' nylon hose—only to have the last package snatched up by the person just in front of them—most individuals were ready to resume a less hectic lifestyle. The populace looked to the leadership of the auctioneer-editor from Lewisburg who had taken his place as head of the state. His down-to-earth personality was surely just what the state needed to steer it back through its reconversion from a time of war to a time of peace.

McCord was born on March 17, 1879, in Bedford County. His Scotch-Irish parents were Thomas N. and Iva Stelle McCord. He was one of the couple's eleven children (and a twin, but his brother died). He spent his childhood helping out on the family farm and attending the area school, and in early manhood he was elected mayor of Lewisburg, serving thirteen terms. The rural voters of his eleven-county district sent him to Congress in 1942, and two years later he won the governor's chair. In 1944, he became the first Democratic candidate for governor to run without opposition in the party primary.

McCord's leading achievement during his initial term was in obtaining an increase in appropriations for public schools by enacting the first state sales tax program (2 percent on the dollar). Crump in Memphis opposed the measure, and McCord led a motor caravan all the way to Memphis to persuade the political dictator to give up his opposition to the sales tax. His trip was successful, and the 2 percent tax went into effect in 1947. By that law and the establishment of a state retirement law for teachers and other state employees, McCord earned a place as one of the strongest friends of education in the history of the state.

In spite of the horde of returning veterans who had to be assimilated, and the passage of the G.I. Bill of Rights in Congress, which took priority on the agenda of government along about this time, in Tennessee the passage of the educational expansion program in the 1947 legislature gave McCord his status as governor. The new state revenues made possible Tennessee's first comprehensive minimum school program for grades one through twelve. It provided for new school buildings and buses throughout the ninety-five counties without additional expense of county and city, aided state colleges, brought a raise in pay to teachers as well as annual leaves and sick benefits, and laid a solid foundation for employment of more than 20,000 teachers in the state. The blind, dependent children, and the aged were to also benefit from the tax.

But in spite of its advantages, the sales tax blanket was received as a sort of child-terrible by much of the populace, and they determined to throw it off by usurping McCord in his third bid for office.

Labor, a growing political strength, also gave McCord trouble, for he had signed an open shop or "right to work" bill, which brought strong criticism. This opposition plus the general attitude regarding the sales tax ousted McCord from the governorship in 1948. Tennesseans voted again for Gordon Browning, who had served the state one term already (1937-39). Estes Kefauver was elected senator in this same year, and it was in this election that the Crump machine, in its effort to prevent the election of Kefauver, met its defeat. (McCord, too, had Crump's backing, and this fact alone was weight enough to tip the scales toward McCord's opponent, Gordon Browning).

It seems a strange twist of fate that the governor who had gone the way of the politician without formal education should score the highest of any governor as the provider for that institution. But McCord was not an unlearned man. He was self-taught, both from volumes in his brother's bookstore at Shelbyville where he worked and read and from the general populace, where he learned congeniality and the rudiments of the political handshake.

He had not forgotten the soil, however, and kept one foot on the land with an interest in cattle auctioneering.

McCord officiated at many livestock auctions, particularly of Jersey cattle (his own special interest), and cried the sales of community and civic fund-raising projects as well, where his proficient old-time oratory, forgotten almost now in the state, brought renewed appreciation from his listeners.

He acquired the *Marshall County Gazette,* where he was active for many years as owner and publisher, and served in the capacity of president for numerous organizations, including the American Jersey Breeders' Association, for which he was also an auctioneer. He is recorded as having flown to Columbus, Ohio (without his political associates' knowledge) during his gubernatorial campaign to conduct a sale for the association. For three years, he headed the Tennessee Printing Commission, and served as president of the Middle Tennessee Press Association for one year. Added to these activities were his obligations to his lay positions in the First Presbyterian Church in Lewisburg where he was an elder and a teacher of a men's Bible class, and whatever duties a 32nd Degree Scottish Rite Masonic position would place upon him.

Much credit is given McCord for his help in fostering the registry society for Tennessee walking horses in 1935. When the Tennessee Walking Horse Breeders Association of America was formed, Jim Nance McCord was its first secretary-treasurer.

After his defeat for a third term, he returned once again to his newspaper in Marshall County, where he and the first Mrs. McCord continued to share civic and church interests.

In 1901 he had married Vera Kercheval, daughter of W. K. and Mollie McKinney Kercheval of Lewisburg. They had no children, and she died in 1953. In 1954, he married Mrs. John Arthur Sheeley, of Paris, Tennessee, who died in 1966. The following year, at eighty-eight, the ex-governor married Mrs. T. Howard Estes of Nashville. McCord died the following year on September 2. He was buried in Lone Oak Cemetery at Lewisburg. He left no descendants.

F R A N K   G O A D   C L E M E N T
(Democrat)
(1953-59; 1963-67)

The old orators were gone from Tennessee in 1953, but Frank Clement, with his podium eloquence, proved a good substitute and became the state's second youngest governor. He had made it his business to lounge against the farmers' haystacks and truckbeds, or to stand erect in tails at stately banquets, and he saw to it that he fit in either situation. Hence in the 1952 Democratic primaries, Governor Browning learned that he was to be unseated the following year by the upcoming young lawyer from Dickson. In the same year, the aged Senator McKellar (after thirty-six years in the Senate) experienced defeat by the young Democratic Congressman, Albert Gore of Carthage. But for the first time since 1928, the state voted for a Republican president (Eisenhower).

Under the young governor, Tennessee would make its first constitutional changes since 1870. In April 21, 1953, the constitutional convention assembled in Nashville with former governor Prentice Cooper (who had returned to the state after serving as an ambassador to Peru) as chairman. Another ex-governor, Ben W. Hooper, was vice-chairman. Among the revisions to be made in the state's eighty-three-year-old laws were amendments to raise the pay of legislators from $4.00 to $15.00 per day and authorize later changes by legislative action to increase the governor's term from two to four years (but he would by the same amendment be ineligible for immediate reelection), to give the governor power to veto individual items of appropriation bills, (but

Frank Goad Clement
1953-1959, 1963-1967

end his use of the pocket veto), to make unconstitutional a poll tax (which had already been abolished in legislative action), to prohibit so-called "ripper" bills (bills that would change the structure of local government without any consideration being given to the wishes of inhabitants), to authorize home rule for cities, and to authorize consolidation of city and county functions.

During Governor Clement's administration, a bond issue was authorized to finance free textbooks in all twelve grades in public schools (previous issue of textbooks had applied to lower grades only); an improved mental health program was inaugurated; and Tennessee's new $2.5 million State Library and Archives Building was opened. And as fate—that pedagogue in irony—would have it, the voters who had complained at the two-cent sales tax under McCord would find themselves confronted with a three-cent tax under Clement, for the cost of state upkeep, like that of the homes, had headed upward.

In 1957, integration laws had come to the land, and that boiling pot of human rights was a heated issue across the state. The legislature passed five school segregation statutes, though not necessarily instigated by Governor Clement. The most important one, a parents' preference law, was declared unconstitutional by a federal district court, thus opening the way for the gradual integration plan. The teachers' retirement law was amended so as to authorize coverage under the federal social security program; and consolidated metropolitan governments were authorized, which later led to the creation of the metropolitan district of Nashville and Davidson County.

Clement started the first hospitalization program for the state's indigent, created its first speech and hearing center, established a special commission for youth guidance and for alcoholism, and started the first long-range highway program within the state.

Frank Clement was born on June 2, 1920, in Dickson, the son of Robert S. and Maybelle Goad Clement. His father was a lawyer and a city judge in Dickson, and his grandfather had been a state senator. After graduating from Central High School in Dickson in 1937, Clement attended Cumberland University in Lebanon for two years, and then transferred to Vanderbilt University where he received the LL.B. degree in June, 1942. One year before he was graduated, he passed the state bar examination, and during 1941 and 1942 he practiced law and attended school at the same time.

By age twenty-three, Clement had received a position with the F.B.I., working in the Chicago area. But the world again trembled under the quake of war, and the young Volunteer entered Officers Candidate School eventually receiving a commission as a second lieutenant. He did not see service overseas, and was discharged in March, 1946.

Practicing law again in Dickson, Clement became counsel for the State Public Service Commission where, at twenty-six, he attracted statewide attention by winning for Tennessee a notable telephone-rate victory and saving the taxpayer's pocketbooks. The voters took note of such contributions and elected him governor in 1953.

But Clement had let them know he was on his way. He had been recalled to the army in 1950 and had spent sixteen months at Camp Gordon, Georgia, as an instructor. Even while serving there, he had kept his growing political organization in Tennessee intact. Prior to his discharge again in 1951, Clement had announced he would be a candidate for governor in 1952. He had already shown his strength as an orator and an organizer, and now he was ready to step to the front as the state's governor.

Following World War II and again the Korean conflict, the populace looked within themselves and to their leaders for strength. They were confronted with realities as never

before, and some recalled previous reports that professors
at Vanderbilt University were encouraging thoughts that
contradicted biblical teachings. The fundamentalists dubbed
Vanderbilt a "hotbed of Modernism" whose professors, with
their encouragement of scientific thought, would "under-
mine the faith of the fathers." [16]

And possibly because the common people felt a need
of one more powerful than themselves to intervene in
settling domestic and foreign affairs, a powerful evangelistic movement swept the state during the 1950s and 1960s,
and churches experienced new growth. In such an atmosphere, Billy Graham, the noted evangelistic orator, found a
welcome in Tennessee in both 1951 and 1954, and Governor Clement is recorded as having developed a warm
friendship with the crusader. At the onset of Clement's
term, on April 1, 1953, the Reverend Graham addressed
the Tennessee General Assembly.

Having been chosen by the United States Junior
Chamber of Commerce in 1949 as one of the ten outstanding young men of the nation, Governor Clement
found himself selected to head many organizations. He was
selected as chairman of the Cordell Hull Foundation—
named in honor of that Tennessean who received the
Nobel Peace Prize for his part in the creation of the United
Nations—and toured ten South American countries in
behalf of the Hull Foundation's efforts of international
education. He was requested to deliver the keynote address
at the 1956 National Democratic Convention where his
rhetoric captured the attention of a nationwide listening
audience.

Clement and his wife (the former Lucille Christenson,
daughter of Houston County judge Nelson Christenson, a
notable politician in the Democratic party) toured Europe.

[16]Folmsbee, et. al., *Tennessee: A Short History,* 556.

The governor came home with the words that communism had an unalterable goal—that of world dominance—and that democracy should constantly guard against its threat.

At the end of Governor Clement's second term (the first had been a two-year term and the second a four-year term), Buford Ellington, who had served as campaign manager for Clement in his gubernatorial races in 1952 and 1954, and who held the position of commissioner of agriculture under the young governor, followed him into the governor's chair.

Entering law again in Nashville, Clement bided his time, for by provisions of the constitution, he could not immediately succeed himself after his second term. When the time was right (1963), he returned to the high office and served another four-year term. He remained at the state's head longer than any other governor, with the exceptions of John Sevier and William Carroll. However, in spite of his record as governor, he later failed in two attempts to win a place in the U.S. Senate.

It seems a gross error of fate that a life so forceful as that of Frank Clement should be paralleled in death by an equal force. On November 4, 1969, the forty-nine-year-old ex-governor was killed in an automobile accident near Nashville. He was buried in Dickson Memorial Gardens.

Three sons bear his name. He was Methodist, a 32nd Degree Mason, and a Shriner.

BUFORD ELLINGTON
(Democrat)
(1959-1963; 1967-1971)

The Democrats elected Buford Ellington, a Tennessee farmer and merchant, to succeed Governor Clement. For eighteen years, the Clement-Ellington factor of the Democratic party would dominate the state's power structure.

(Clement had been the first governor in Tennessee's history to serve a four-year term, allowable under the constitutional change of 1953.) Ellington's main pledge—no increase in taxes—was music to the ears of Tennesseans. At the end of his four-year term, however, Clement was again elected; Ellington took his second turn again in 1967, following Clement's term.

Folks called it the "leap frog" government, and took the turnover in stride. But it should be noted here as well that the two men had apparently cooled toward one another by the end of their eight-year coalition. In the 1960 presidential election, Ellington, chairman of the National Democratic Convention (the first Tennessee governor to have that honor), led a 33-man delegation in support of Lyndon Johnson, while Clement supported John F. Kennedy.

Ellington was born in Holmes County, Mississippi, on June 27, 1907, the son of A. E. and Cora Ellington. He attended the local school at Goodman, Mississippi, and then entered Millsaps College in Jackson, where he studied religion. Working his way as he went, he started editing a weekly newspaper in Durant. There he met and married Catherine Cheek, daughter of James and Fannie Bell Cheek of Marshall County, Tennessee. Miss Cheek was a teacher in the Durant School.

At heart Ellington was a man-of-the-soil. He liked the Tennessee hills and the farming land in Marshall County. Ten years after his marriage, he bought a general store at Verona and moved his family there.

Ellington spent eight years as a salesman for International Harvester Company in Memphis, and knew the role of the merchant. That step as a merchant would prove worthwhile on his way to the governor's chair. A knowledge of agriculture was not to be overlooked in political utility, as Ellington was to discover.

Buford Ellington
1959-1963, 1967-1971

He bought a farm in 1942 and started the ground-work—whether to his knowledge or not—for a political career. Many were the hands he would clasp as he traveled over the state supervising a sales force for the Tennessee Farm Bureau Insurance System.

He supported Jim McCord in his bid for Congress and then for governor, and was Marshall County campaign manager for Joe Evins in 1946. By 1948, Ellington had been elected to the legislature from Marshall County, and in 1952 headed the Clement campaign that unseated Browning and put Clement in the governor's chair.

In the Clement administration, Ellington was known as the governor's chief lieutenant and advisor; but he was also the agriculture commissioner and won distinction in eradicating brucellosis as a threat to Tennessee cattle. He founded an agricultural diagnostic laboratory at Nashville which is named in his honor.

Under Ellington, the state constitution saw another alteration made in the convention of July, 1959, which was authorized by the governor and the voters. This limited convention extended county office-holders' terms to four years, and went into effect on September 1, 1962.

By 1965, the constitution was again amended, proposing four-year staggered terms for senators, the apportionment of the Assembly on the basis of population, the division of counties into districts in those counties having two or more representatives or two or more senators, the calling of special sessions if two-thirds of each house so requested (as well as by the governor, as previously provided), "split" sessions of the legislature, and annual salaries for legislators. These proposals were adopted in 1966.

After four years in office, Ellington went the way of many of his predecessors upon leaving the governorship, becoming associated with the railroads. He took the position of vice-president of the Louisville-Nashville Railroad, but put the job aside shortly thereafter and worked with the civil rights movement at President Johnson's appointment as the state sought adjustment from segregation mores that had bound it for well over a century.

During his first campaign and hence his first term as governor, Ellington had deemed himself an old-fashioned segregationist from Mississippi. At the onset of his 1966 campaign, however, in the heat of the civil rights controversy, he announced that he had been wrong in his first opinion and proded desegregation along by appointing H. T. Lacard of Memphis, a Negro, into his cabinet as an administrative assistant.

Ellington also formed the Tennessee Human Relations Commission, and took other steps designed to appeal to blacks. Truly the progress of the state in such direction could be felt as individuals paid tribute on the national day of mourning for Dr. Martin Luther King, the black civil rights leader who met an assassin's bullet at Memphis on April 4, 1968.

As governor, Ellington sponsored a $900 million state budget, which included a $100 annual raise for school teachers during each year of the 1959-61 biennium. He reorganized the state government, cutting the number of departments drastically and placing independent regulatory boards under department jurisdiction in much the same manner as Governor Peay had done in 1923, for waste had a way of slipping into government.

Under his administration. the state repealed the Anti-Evolution Law of 1925, which had been the occasion for the historic "monkey trial" in Dayton. The county-option system of 1939 for liquor regulation was amended so as to permit cities in dry counties to hold referendums on the legalization of "package stores," and the urban counties were given the opportunity to legalize the sale of liquor by the drink. But an effort to repeal what was left of the state's "bone-dry" law failed during the session of 1968.

Ellington's second term saw the end of the Clement-Ellington alternations. Clement had been the victim of a fatal automobile accident in 1969. Ellington died suddenly while playing golf in Florida on April 3, 1972. His body was flown back to the state for burial at Lone Oak Cemetery in Lewisburg.

A Methodist and a 33rd Degree Scottish Rite Mason, Ellington served as trustee of the University of Tennessee, Peabody College, and Rust College of Holly Springs, Mississippi, and as a director of the Millsaps College Alumni Association.

He left a son and a daughter.

WINFIELD C. DUNN
(Republican)
(1971-1975)

It was young Memphis dentist Winfield Dunn who broke the regime of Democratic governorship in Tennessee in 1971. He became the first Republican governor in fifty years to head the state. Under the capable steering of this campaign manager, Lamar Alexander (who would himself oppose Ray Blanton in the next gubernatorial election), Dunn swept into the governor's chair from relative political obscurity, promising Tennesseans that his administration was to be one of partnership, not partisanship, and pledged his reign as a new era of citizen participation in the governmental affairs of Tennessee.

Vowing to take the government of the people to the people, and emphasizing unity for the state, the new Republican governor contended: "Unity is the bedrock of our strength...and I will constantly encourage the attitude that we are truly the one great state—not the three states—

Winfield C. Dunn
1971-1975

of Tennessee," implying some hope of ridding the state of sectionalism.[17]

A Sunday school teacher in a Methodist church and the father of three, and with youth still an attribute of his own, Dunn favored the eighteen-year-old vote, and encouraged youth groups of the state to become more involved in government.

Republican victory over a half-century of Democratic incumbency resulted in one of the most celebrated inaugurals in Tennessee history. In celebration, more than 1,400 persons launched the three days of inaugural activities that would include three balls, a $100-a-plate dinner at the Municipal Auditorium, and country music from "Music City's" most celebrated entertainers. The inaugural day (January 16) began for the Dunns in church with early morning prayer activities and culminated with better than 5,000 persons attending the reception later at the governor's mansion.

Winfield Dunn was born in Meridian, Mississippi, on July 1, 1927, to Aubert C. and Dorothy Crum Dunn. He was educated in the area schools and at age seventeen—in the true spirit of the state that he was to head—was a volunteer in that throng of American youths who packed trains and buses and left their small towns all across the land to join the fight against Nazism in World War II. Dunn chose the U. S. Navy, and served overseas as a pharmacist's mate during 1945 and 1946.

After the war, Dunn earned a degree in banking and finance at the University of Mississippi, but not satisfied in that area, attended the School of Dentistry at the University of Tennessee in Memphis where he earned a doctorate in dental surgery. He first entered a dental practice with his father-in-law, and later opened his own office.

[17]*Nashville Banner,* January 16, 1971, p. 1.

In 1950 he had married Betty Jane Prichard, daughter of Dr. Frank and Ruby Howell Prichard. Miss Prichard was a student at Ole Miss, and Dunn was then engaged in the insurance business. A short while after their marriage, they returned to Memphis where Mrs. Dunn taught school while the governor-to-be studied the dentistry profession.

Unlike practically all other governors of Tennessee, Dunn did not serve in the legislature, but he was a personable civic leader in Memphis. He was chairman of the Republican party of Shelby County, and was awarded an honorary Juris Doctorate from Southwestern University in Memphis.

Dunn was active in his support of community organizations, fraternity and professional organizations, boys' clubs, Jaycees, etc., in sympathy with their needs and pleading their causes. With such a background and the careful planning of his gubernatorial campaign, he became the governor of Tennessee in 1971.

The state's population was reported at 3,924,164 in 1970, and already the "freeways" groaned in efforts to circle the cities. The agrarian culture of the century's beginning was far removed from the major part of the state when Dunn forsook his adjustable dental chair for the chair in back of the governor's desk. Tennessee, like the other states, faced urbanization, and had for several years already, that meant problems not brought to it before. Ten years earlier, Governor Ellington had created the Department of Conservation and Commerce with a greatly expanded program for industrial development, and Nashville had experienced a hearty growth from the various industries.

Racial strife had troubled the state for well over a decade with "sit-ins" and "freedom riders" bringing to focus the "second-class citizenship to which Negroes were subjected." [18] Civil rights leaders had urged non-violence in their long pursuit of human equality, but such forceful social movements demand the dues of the debtor, and numerous buildings in Memphis, Nashville, Chattanooga, and other cities across the state were looted and burned. Financial damages proved phenomenal to the state, and so did damages to human relationships.

But after the dramatic assassination of Dr. Martin Luther King in Memphis, the state took on new insights. Negroes had been drawn into government and into white schools (and whites into black schools) as education continued in its effort at growth. Whether significant to progress in racial relations or to the times, 1974 saw the close of the Race Relations Information Center in Nashville.

As governor, Dunn continued those trends in education, and developed a statewide kindergarten program. In other areas, he extended the highway construction program to an all-time high, won accreditation of mental health institutions, reorganized the major branches of state government, initiated the regional prison concept, created the Department of Economic and Community Development, implemented a long-range planning program for the state, initiated a primary health care program in the Department of Health, and saw issue of a $30 million capital improvement program for study of health sciences. The state constitution was altered again in 1972 in a convention at Nashville, with the only change being the order of a classified property tax. Tennessee was declared a disaster area as tornadoes ripped away lives and property in the spring of 1974.

The Democrats regained the gubernatorial office again in 1975, and Winfield Dunn was followed in the coveted position by Ray Blanton. After leaving the governor's chair,

[18]Folmsbee, et. al., *Tennessee: A Short History*, 575.

Dr. Dunn took a position with the Hospital Corporation of America in Nashville where he serves as vice-president of public relations. The only ex-governor living, he and his family live in Nashville.

While governor, Dunn was twice elected to the Executive Committee of the National Governors Conference and served as chairman of the Republican Governors Association. He is a former chairman of the Education Commission of the States, the Board of Trustees of the University of Tennessee, the Tennessee Board of Regents, and the Tennessee-Tombigbee Waterway Development Authority.

Whether Dunn will attempt the second series of "leap frog" government in opposition to the Democrats in the next gubernatorial election remains to be seen. Judging from the other governors who started their ascensions up the political ladder, one rung for him may not be enough.

Dr. Dunn is a Methodist, a Mason, and a Shriner. He is a member of the American Legion and maintains his professional status with state and national dental associations. He serves in an advisory capacity to various national organizations, including the Department of Health, Education and Welfare. He has three times been chosen Tennessee man of the year.

RAY BLANTON
(Democrat)
(1975-1979)

The Republican victory of 1970 was short-lived, with Ray Blanton of west Tennessee winning the governor's chair in 1975. He had entered the primary early, winning the nomination for Tennessee's forty-fourth governor over eleven other candidates. In the general election, he defeated Republican Lamar Alexander, who had so successfully managed Governor Dunn's Republican campaign in 1970.

Born to Leonard and Ova Delaney Blanton in Harden County on April 10, 1930, Ray Blanton arrived with the Great Depression. As a farm youth, by age twelve he had planted and harvested his first cotton crop.

He was educated in Hardin County Schools, and received a Danforth Foundation Award for outstanding scholarship while attending the Old Shiloh High School. Following his graduation, he took a job as a grocery clerk and worked his way through the University of Tennessee, earning a B.S. degree in agriculture and chemistry.

While at the university, Blanton married Betty Littlefield, daughter of Henry and Maxie Littlefield of Adamsville. After earning his degree, he and his wife moved to Indiana, where he taught school for a year.

Returning to Tennessee, he helped form a road-construction business called B & B Construction Company with his brother Gene and their father, a former mayor of Adamsville. Serving as executive with the company and exercising an avid interest in community and civic affairs in his hometown, Ray Blanton was already oriented toward political life, and following the charted route for executive office, he was sent by the voters in Chester and McNairy Counties to the legislature in 1964.

Setting his sight higher, he ran successfully for the U.S. Congress in 1966, and was elected for two additional terms. As a congressman, he spoke at every high school and college in his district, and every year sent each high-school graduate a booklet entitled *How to Finance Your College*, published at his own expense. He also conducted "Hot Line" programs with schools through a special telephone hookup.

Challenging Republican senator Howard Baker for his seat in 1972, Ray Blanton suffered his first political setback in a traumatic election in which Republicans won landslide victories in Tennessee, as well as across the nation.

Although observers predicted Blanton's career was at an end, he immediately began laying plans for the 1974

Ray Blanton
1975-1979

gubernatorial election, in which he defeated his Republican opponent Lamar Alexander.

Blanton's inauguration took place in January 1975, and he started his term with the 89th General Assembly of Tennessee, attempting yet, almost two centuries since the state government had been formed, to guide the state toward progressiveness and stability.

His administration saw the first major revision of the state's franchise and excise laws since 1937; made a revision in the Hall Income Tax to provide relief to citizens sixty-five years of age and older who fell within fixed income designations; instigated consumer-protection insurance policies; and passed the Restitution Centers Act, which would allow prisoners who committed lesser felonies to hold jobs away from prisons in order to support their dependents, pay court costs at trials, and provide financial restitution to the victims of their crimes.

He created the Department of Tourism—the first in the nation—and Tennessee was the first state to raise tourism to a cabinet-level department.

Traveling extensively for the state, making numerous trips to Washington, D.C., and overseas to recruit foreign investments, he was criticized for his large travel expenses. But interests of British, Japanese, and German investors paid large dividends in industries brought into the state, providing jobs for Tennesseans.

Regarding the state budget, Blanton revealed satisfaction at his administration's accomplishments in areas of physical responsibilities and budget reform, stating that in a time of severe economic recession, he had been able to keep the budget balanced and maintained.

Through his personal involvement in agriculture, Blanton was responsive to agrarian problems and supported higher farm parity, together with protection for family farms.

He avowed concerns for the needs of education while

that institution faced a period of emphases on extracurricular activities as it was leaving the basics in education and attempting to educate the "whole" child, in contrast to that old school model, which stressed the three "R's."

Blanton urged Tennesseans not to be satisfied with the state's traditional low rating in education, insisting that the true measure of that entity was not in dollars spent but in what the student gained from his teachers. And he appealed to Tennessee-trained teachers to remain in the state, rather than to seek employment outside its borders.

Like Dunn before him, he placed much emphasis on the youth of the state. He was strong in his support of youth-oriented programs, and helped to force through passage of the bill that gave eighteen-year-olds the right to vote.

He joined the legislature in upgrading the state's retirement program and emphasized programs promoting equality for women and African Americans. Under Blanton's reign, Tennesseans' taxes went down because the state's credit rating went up.

So then how, one would ask, or why, with such worthy aspirations for the state he governed, would this governor—even though heavily in debt from a bad oil well investment—look away from the high road, take the path to destruction and find himself toppled from the lofty nest, cutting short his term in the governor's chair by three days? He was ousted from office, his office door was nailed shut—to protect evidence of wrongdoing—and his successor, Lamar Alexander, was sworn into office three days early.

By the day of such, his administration—which had been labeled one of the most controversial in the state's history—had been deemed corrupt. Blanton had granted numerous pardons to criminals, and was accused of selling the pardons, though he denied having done so.

But the state's Pardons and Paroles Board chairwoman, Marie Ragghianti, a Blanton appointee, had complained at the release of convicted felons. When she refused to release certain prisoners who—as later events proved—had bribed members of the Blanton administration, Blanton ousted her from her job.

Marie Ragghianti didn't take her dismissal lightly, and retained Fred Thompson, who later become a U.S. Senator from Tennessee, as her lawyer. In 1978, a Chancery Court jury decided Blanton acted "arbitrarily and capriciously" in firing Ragghianti. She was ordered reinstated, and won a $38,000 settlement in back pay from the state, though she never returned to the job.

Peter Maas brought her story to national attention in the book *Marie*, which became a movie starring actress Sissy Spacek in the role of Ragghianti. Fred Thompson played himself.

Although Blanton stated that he had not profited from the pardon deals himself, he was allowing the illegal activity by pardoning prisoners recommended for such by his aides—who were profiting from the clemency exchange. His legal counsel had earlier been arrested with marked bills from a pardon sale.

This cash-for-clemency scandal broke on December 15, 1978, the day after Blanton had held a Christmas celebration at the stately Executive Residence in the posh area of Oak Hill in Nashville for his commissioners and staff. There the group presented him with a surprise Christmas gift—a metallic-blue Lincoln Continental.

In the early afternoon on December 15, he received a frantic call at the Executive Residence from his press secretary, informing him that FBI agents had swarmed the Capitol and were inside the office of his legal counsel T. Edward Sisk, with the doors locked.

There, they seized hundreds of documents relating to the executive clemency scandal, as well as records from the desk of Blanton's appointment secretary. A short time later, the FBI announced the arrest of Sisk and two other

Blanton aides, one of them a state trooper assigned to Blanton's security staff.

On December 23, Blanton was questioned by a federal grand jury and later told reporters that he had nothing to hide.

On January 15, 1979, with public sentiment growing to remove him from office by swearing in the new Republican governor-in-waiting Lamar Alexander before the scheduled January 20 inauguration, Blanton emerged from a three-hour meeting to announce that he had granted executive clemency to 52 inmates. His stated reason was that he was under court orders to reduce the overcrowded prison population.

One such pardon was issued to a prisoner serving twenty to forty years for the murder of his wife and her male companion. This prisoner, the son of a Blanton patronage leader in east Tennessee, had been allowed to live outside the prison and serve as a state photographer, an act that had already raised the ire of Tennesseans. His pardon elevated their frenzy.

Convinced that Blanton's office was about to sell more pardons, Lt. Gov. John Wilder, House Speaker Ned McWherter, Chief Justice Joe Henry, and Attorney General William Leech, all Democrats, gathered in the Supreme Court Chambers and administered the oath to Lamar Alexander at night. The action was carried into homes in the evening on live television.

Blanton was never convicted of selling pardons, but in June 1981, he found himself convicted of mail fraud, conspiracy, and extortion for selling liquor licenses. He, with a few of his closest friends, had been cornering the retail-liquor store market in Nashville by only awarding liquor licenses to their cronies and to themselves. Hence, they could control the stores directly or force the owners to kick back to them 30 percent of the stores' profits.

For his part in these charges, Blanton served 22 months in a federal penitentiary and is said to have spent the next ten years—from 1986 until his death on November 22, 1996—trying to restore his reputation. Nine of the charges were overturned in 1988, by federal court action.

Nevertheless, Blanton's estate was ordered to pay income tax on $38,334 that he received as kickbacks while governor for helping a constituent obtain a $2.5 million construction loan and a liquor license.

The *Nashville Tennessean,* however, pointed out a few negatives in the Blanton charges, stating that he did *not* take money for releasing prisoners and did *not* take bribes to rig bids on state transportation projects (another accusation), although he bore criticism for his family's road construction company having done business with the state. And the company became enmeshed in a state-wide scandal that led to the indictment and conviction of his brother Gene in 1981.

According to the *Tennessean,* Blanton spent nearly two years in jail for his role in scandals that benefited his friends and close aides much more than himself.

At 66, in ill health with liver disease, Blanton died from heart failure. Records disclose that his marriage with his first wife failed, but at his death he was married to Karen Flint Blanton. He left two sons and a daughter. A Methodist, he was buried at Shiloh, laid to rest in a cherry coffin built to his specifications just months before his death. He was the only Tennessee governor ever ousted from office, and the only one sent to prison for official crimes.

The *Tennessean* also noted that "on the other hand, and in spite of his under-handedness, Ray Blanton was an innovator of state government, and a skilled manager of state money . . ."

ANDREW LAMAR ALEXANDER
(Republican)
(1979-1987)

"I'll tell you how to get elected: don't make any promises, we've heard them all before; just do the best you can;
keep the taxes down; and for heaven's sake, behave your-
self when you get in!"

The above words of advice to Lamar Alexander from a
lady in Hawkins County, Tennessee, are as fitting today as
when he began his 1978 campaign for governor of the
state. He won the governorship after donning a red-and-
black checked flannel shirt and walking 1,020 miles
across the state.

Lamar Alexander has been termed Tennessee's
"Squeaky Clean" governor, though he, too, has received a
bit of finger pointing, reportedly when persons who benefited from his term as governor brought him in to lucrative investment deals.

And he does admit to at least two paddlings in school.

Alexander was born July 3, 1940, in Maryville,
Tennessee, the seat of Blount County, to Andrew Lamar,
Sr., and Floreine Rankin Alexander. Both were east
Tennessee educators. His father was an elementary
school principal, but soon after Lamar Jr.'s birth took a
better-paying job at the Aluminum Company of America
plant, located in the area.

In the early 1940s, Floreine Alexander started a pre-
school for area youngsters, which she operated in the
family's garage, this for twenty years, until school officials
agreed to her suggestion that they establish a public
kindergarten.

When young Lamar reached Maryville High School, he
was active in varsity basketball and tennis, and participated

in debate. Before and after school, he delivered newspapers, and from age three until he reached eighteen, he took piano lessons. He sang in a Presbyterian church choir and says he faithfully attended Sunday school.

With the benefit of a scholarship, he entered Vanderbilt University in Nashville, where he was active in journalism, becoming editor of the university newspaper and using his position to promote racial tolerance. The school had no black undergraduates at that time, and Lamar was a strong advocate of integrating the student body. Upon graduating with membership in Phi Beta Kappa in 1962, he enrolled at the New York University School of Law on a Root-Tilden scholarship. There he served on the Law Review and obtained his LL.B. degree in 1965.

Upon his return to Tennessee, he practiced law briefly with the Knoxville firm of Fowler, Roundtree, Fowler, and Robertson. He then served as a law clerk to Judge John Minor Wisdom of the United States Circuit Court of Appeals for the Fifth District in New Orleans, moonlighting in his off hours as a piano player in local night clubs.

Edging more toward politics, he directed Howard Baker's first successful bid for the Senate, and served as Baker's legislative assistant for two years. On January 4, 1969, he married Leslee Kathryn Buhler, whom he met at a Capitol Hill softball game. He was on the team of Senator Baker's Staff, while she was a member of the team of her boss, the Republican senator John C. Tower of Texas.

In 1970, Lamar returned to Tennessee and directed the gubernatorial campaign of Winfield Dunn, with whom he served as transition coordinator after the election.

Then from 1971 to 1978, Alexander practiced law with the Dearborn and Ewing firm in Nashville, where he helped to establish and head the Tennessee Council on Crime and Delinquency.

But in 1974, he had made a run for the governor's

Andrew Lamar Alexander
(1979-1987)

chair, only to be defeated by Ray Blanton, at a time when anti-Republican backlash caused by the Washington Watergate scandal was rampant. But he was not ready to give up, and kept his name before the voters by delivering public commentary on a Nashville television station for two years.

When Howard Baker became Senate minority leader in 1977, he again hired Alexander as his special counsel, and on January 26, 1978, Alexander kicked off a second campaign for governor, again by embarking on a walk across the state. This time, he spent five months on the thousand-mile walk, again wearing what had become his trademark—a red-and-black checked flannel shirt.

Of the second walk as he criss-crossed the state, he wrote, "The thousand-mile walk, day after day after day, became my metronome, a practiced discipline that infused me with the music of the lives of the people I sought to serve. Living in their homes put me better in tune with myself and with them. I knew I had found my mission. I knew I was in my groove . . ."

He stated that for the first time ever, he felt he possessed that candescence that voters see in a candidate with a purpose. And he won the election, taking over his first governorship at night—three days early.

When federal prosecutors presented him with evidence that Governor Blanton was suspected of plans to issue more paroles to prisoners—above the 52 he had already issued, almost half the prisoners convicted murders—and at the request of the U.S. Attorney, Alexander was sworn in as governor three days ahead of schedule.

On January 17, 1979, he became Tennessee's forty-fifth governor. (He would also be the first chief executive in the state's history to win election to a second term.)

In his first year in office, Alexander succeeded in passing a tough anti-crime program, imposing mandatory

sentences for violent criminals and building more prisons, though the construction plans could not keep pace
with the swelling ranks of inmates.

In the wake of a prison riot in 1985, Thomas A.
Higgins, a United States District Court judge, ordered the
state to ease overcrowding. In order to comply, Alexander
was forced to relax mandatory-sentencing rules pending
the construction of two maximum-security prisons.

By the beginning of his second term in 1983, education had become Lamar Alexander's chief focus, and he
proposed a radical reform of the state's education system.
He tried to push through a plan to tie teacher bonuses to
teacher-student performance, but his plan failed in the
legislature.

Convinced that his idea was sound, he again stumped
the state, organizing citizens' task forces in each district
and compiling signed petitions that urged the legislature
to reconsider his suggestion. Hence, the Comprehensive
Education Reform Act of 1984—commonly called the
Better Schools Program—passed by a narrow margin, and
the $1.2 billion measure improved public schools with
funds generated by a one-cent increase in the state sales
tax, and made possible computers in all junior high
schools.

Under Alexander's leadership, Japanese investment in
Tennessee, already growing under Blanton's administra-
tion, continued to expand, creating thousands of jobs in
"The Volunteer State," especially jobs in the automobile
industry, including those at the Nissan plant at Smyrna.
More auto manufacturing jobs were created with the
announcement of the building of the Saturn plant at
Spring Hill.

Alexander also supported the creation of a Tennessee
Parkway system, which improved highway transportation
and enhanced the state's expanding tourism industry. His

Tennessee Homecoming '86 program was extremely popular, as 812 communities across the state launched special
projects and publications about state and local heritage.

Spurred by federal court decisions mandating change,
he addressed the state's antiquated corrections system
and began a massive prison construction program.

Naturally, a man who has worn so many hats as
Alexander—who is, too, an eloquent writer, with several
books behind him and probably more in front of him—is
bound to wind down sooner or later. And after eight years
in the governor's chair, when he began to sense his children "drifting toward their mother's end of the dinner
table," or so he described the growing distance between
his children and himself, he made up his mind that what
they all needed together was a long vacation. One about
six months long, as it turned out, for on the very day that
he left the office of governor, he, his wife, and their four
children left for a six-month odyssey "down under."

In Australia, they rented a home, bought an Australian
car, and learned to drive on the wrong side. The four children walked to Australian schools and for six months they
all experienced the Australian culture. Alexander wrote
of the family's sojourn in a book titled *Six Months Off, An
American Family's Australian Adventure.* His wife termed
their jaunt a family renewal and simply time to smell the
roses along the way.

Back in private life again, in 1987, Alexander continued his goal of improving education in America. He was
chair of the Leadership Institute at Belmont in 1987-
1988, and from 1988-1991 he served as president of the
University of Tennessee, where he established that institution's first full-year scholarship program and developed a new five-year comprehensive plan for the university system.

There, too, he appointed the university's first black
and first female vice-presidents.

With a reputation for innovation and commitment to education, Alexander was appointed by President George Bush as U.S. secretary of education in 1991. And again, just as Lamar Alexander had followed an ousted governor in the Tennessee governor's chair, so did he, as the country's fifth secretary of education, when President Bush dismissed Lauro Cavazos from that office.

As secretary of education, Alexander initiated and supported administration policy to set voluntary National Educational Standards, to prohibit race-based scholarships at colleges and universities, and to implement America 2000, a program to achieve national educational goals established by President Bush and the nation's governors.

After Bush's defeat in 1992, Alexander returned to Tennessee and was a counsel at the law firm of Baker, Donelson, Bearman, and Caldwell from 1993-1995. He remained active in Republican Party activities as chair of the Republican Exchange Satellite Network from 1993-1995.

On February 28, 1995, he launched a campaign for the Republican presidential nomination, but after faring poorly in the early primaries, he withdrew in the spring of 1996.

An attorney, writer, and Republican party leader, Alexander presently lives in Nashville.

NED RAY MCWHERTER
(Democrat)
(1987-1995)

If Lamar Alexander's checked flannel shirt symbolized to Tennessee Republicans that he wanted to be one of them, then Ned McWherter's lifted coffee cup and a handful of vanilla wafers was symbolic to Tennessee Democrats of McWherter's campaign promise to be a "working first-day chief executive."

"Swear me in, give me four vanilla wafers and a cup of coffee, and I'll be ready to go to work," he had maintained, while campaigning for the chair that two-term Lamar Alexander was leaving.

An estimated eight thousand supporters on the Legislative Plaza at Nashville would join McWherter in the cookie festival that day, where Nabisco had provided the Democratic inauguration with 20,000 miniature packages of vanilla wafers, soon grabbed up by the handfuls. The front of the packages bore a silver decal with McWherter's campaign motto—"Our best is yet to come."

Bands from the University of Tennessee and Tennessee's National Guard performed in grand style as McWherter—sharecropper's son, short-order cook, shoe salesman, trucker, beer distributor, farmer, and legislative leader—prepared to take on his new title as Tennessee's forty-sixth governor.

On the steps of the War Memorial Auditorium, surrounded by the state's political notables and numerous supporters, he did so.

Predictions of rain failed to dampen the spirits of Democrats waiting to reclaim the statehouse after eight years of Republican rule. The night before, an estimated fifteen thousand Democrats had celebrated this return in three separate balls at the Opryland Hotel, with McWherter dropping by each of them.

Following his inaugural oath, McWherter escorted his cabinet members and senior staff to the House chamber, where he had presided for the past fourteen years. There, they each repeated a separate oath of office. Then, in the crisp air and under gray skies, McWherter returned to the Plaza reviewing stand to watch a parade that included units from all ninety-five Tennessee counties.

Soon, Governor Lamar Alexander, about to head out for Australia with his family, would salute his friend and successor in a short-short speech before turning his place of eight years over to McWherter, whose day it truly was, and whose supporters this day wore red inaugural buttons hawked by

Ned Ray McWherter
(1987-1995)

the president of Political Americana, specializing in campaign buttons for collectors and Democratic candidates.

After acknowledging his seventy-six-year-old mother, seated on the first row of the platform, who McWherter said had taught him right from wrong, and had always been there for him, in the good times and in the hard times (his father had died ten years earlier); and after his good words for outgoing Governor Lamar Alexander, McWherter, in his eleven-minute inaugural speech, stressed community pride, optimism, and fairness.

He told Tennesseans he would have them all as family, that no group or region would be favored, and that none would be forgotten.

In an impressive comparison between state and family, he said that no state that chose to ignore its troubled regions and people while watching others thrive could call itself justified, and no family that favored its strong children, or failed to help a child in trouble, would be worthy of the name.

This might have been expected from this governor's family, who, as he sought the executive office, had all pitched in to do their share. His son, Mike McWherter, left his position with the Nashville law firm of Donelson, Stokes, and Bartholomew for a while to devote his full time to campaigning for his father, traveling back and forth across the state.

McWherter's daughter, Linda Ramsey, mother of two sons and a physical education instructor at the university level, took time out of her busy schedule to do the same, accompanying her grandmother Lucille McWherter on campaign appearances and hosting a series of "Teas for Tennessee" across the state on behalf of her father. She also is credited with coordinating the "McWherter Mile," in the Hands Across America fund drive for the hungry and homeless, raising more than $13,000 for the project.

Ned McWherter was born in Palmersville, of Weakly

County, to Harmon Ray and Lucille Golden Smith McWherter in 1930. At the time, his parents were share-croppers. He was educated in the public schools of Dresden, the seat of Weakly County. In 1948, he joined the Tennessee National Guard and served until 1969, when he retired with the rank of captain.

As a young man, McWherter owned and operated sev-eral businesses while also managing a family farm. Along with his businesses, he became active in civic groups and Democratic politics. In 1968, he won the Democratic nom-ination to represent Lake, Obion, and Weakly Counties in the Tennessee House of Representatives, where his integrity and political shrewdness gained respect.

In 1973, at age 42, he was elected speaker of the house, and he remained in that position until his inauguration as governor in 1987. His seven terms in the House is the longest period there of any speaker in Tennessee history.

As speaker, he presided over all sessions of the House, appointed all committees and committee officers, and largely worked with Republican governors, except during the term of fellow Democrat and west Tennessean Ray Blanton from 1975 to 1979. McWherter appointed the first African-American chairs in the South and assisted women legislators in gaining leadership roles in the House.

His legislative successes included passage of the state "Sunshine Law," which opened all governmental meetings and records to the public, along with new campaign finan-cial disclosure laws. He pioneered the concept of open government in Tennessee. His philosophy was that the public's business should always be transacted in public, and his open-door policy gave all citizens access to him.

McWherter made a strong commitment to the state's educational needs. In the 1980s he had worked closely with Governor Lamar Alexander to reform and enhance the state's public educational system and the state prison system.

He helped enact the revolutionary 21st Century

Schools education reform policy in 1992, with the goal of renewing Tennessee's position of national leadership in education reform in such areas as accountability, performance standards, and the equalizations of funds between rich and poor regions of the state. The program would also provide major new financial support for all schools, from kindergarten through higher education institutions.

His support in recruiting new industries from other nations as well as maintaining and encouraging industry nationally and locally has helped Tennessee to become known throughout the world as a premier business location.

With a large road-building budget, he opened up the potential for building new communities and gave his support to economically depressed communities by creating a state-funded program to build needed facilities to attract industry and jobs.

He initiated the first state-financed program for low-income housing, started community-based Drug Free Tennessee organizations to attack the problems of drug and alcohol abuse, and encouraged innovative solutions to the issue of available and affordable health care in the state.

McWherter brought an innovative management style to state government, allowing him to extend services to the public, make new investments in education and economic development, and keep the state's budget balanced. Magazines that have rated physical management in all the states have consistently rated Tennessee among the best.

His innovative reform of the state Medicaid system, the TennCare program, has been monitored carefully by officials from other states interested in new programs that provide health care for needy citizens at a reasonable public cost.

In 1995, McWherter retired from political office, but remains active in Democrat politics both in Tennessee and at the national level, occasionally providing advice to

President Bill Clinton, whom he has known since Clinton was governor of Arkansas.

Ned McWherter lives in Dresden. He remains a member of a number of civil organizations, and is active in the Southern Speakers Conference, an organization that includes the House speakers of fifteen Southern states.

A Methodist, he was married to the late Bette Jean Beck McWherter.

DON SUNDQUIST
(Republican)
(January 1995 through present)

As a small businessman in Memphis, Governor Sundquist first ran for public office in 1982, after he and his wife Martha Swanson Sundquist, whom he had met while attending Augustana College in Illinois, had raised their three children. They had married in 1959, after she had graduated magna cum laude and he had finished a two-year stint in the U.S. Navy.

With little name recognition of his own, he defied the odds and won the Seventh District congressional seat. He was reelected congressman five times, by support from Republicans, Democrats, and independents.

After twelve years in Washington, he returned home to seek the governorship of Tennessee, winning a hard-fought election that brought together Tennesseans from all walks of life to support his "In Touch With Tennessee" campaign.

In his inaugural address, he stated

"no one should think that government alone is the author of progress in this state. This is the home of Davy Crockett, Sequoyah, Nancy Ward, Alvin York . . . Alex Haley . . . Elvis and Minnie and Dinah, and countless other Tennesseans who have enriched and inspired the lives of millions throughout the world.

I entered public service after having built a
business, raised a family, served my community
and my church (Lutheran), and lived a fulfill-
ing life of private pursuits for forty-six years.

I know that real heroes of our time are not
governors and presidents, but parents, farmers,
teachers, ministers, athletes, soldiers, the people who make the cars we drive and the music
we love, the people who care for those in need
and never get—or expect—a bit of credit. My
faith is not in government but in people. My
goal is for every family to write its own story of
success, large or small, in the soil of Tennessee."

He also spoke of looking forward to his challenges,
adding

"I will lift my eyes unto the hills from which
cometh my help. My help cometh from the
Lord."

"Trusting always in Him, let us rely as well
on ourselves and one another . . . and the
resourceful spirit of the pioneer that lives in all
of us."

Under the sound of his voice, listeners knew that a
true Tennessean was speaking to them. Under his leadership, Tennessee residents, in general, have prospered.

Job growth in the state has continued, and he says the
state is fast approaching a 200,000 new job figure over the
last four years. He adds that from 1990 through 1997,
there were only two other states in which the per capita
income increased at a greater rate than in Tennessee.

Admitting such success can be difficult, he attributes the
record, at least in part, to Tennessee lawmakers who tend to
work together. "This is a bipartisan state," he emphasized.
"We have a government that works. People come to this
state to locate plants and invest here because of that."

He began learning about bipartisan politics at an early

Don Sundquist
(January 1995 through present)

age, when managing Howard Baker's first—and unsuccessful—bid for U.S. Senate in 1964. The experience led
to Sundquist joining the Young Republicans, in which he
later served as both state and national chair.

In 1972, he moved to Memphis and opened his own
business, becoming president and partner of Graphic
Sales of America, a printing and advertising firm. In 1979,
Baker, by then a U.S. Senator, asked him to again manage
his presidential campaign office. Sundquist took a month
off from his business to do so, but ended up working on
the campaign for eight months, and credits Howard
Baker for sparking his interest in politics. Following the
end of the Baker campaign, Sundquist returned to
Memphis, and successfully ran for the U.S. House of
Representatives in 1982, serving six terms.

In 1994, he was elected governor of the state, and was
reelected in 1998.

As the present governor, he is a member of the
Southern Governors' Association, and was elected to a
one-year term as SGA's president. Serving in that capacity, and having kept abreast of changing times, he has
encouraged the entire South to lead the nation in developing telemedicine, a medical practice in which patients
can "see" doctors from miles away.

He explains that patients visit a clinic and sit before a live
television camera, while doctors far from them can observe
them on a television screen. Through two-way voice com-
munications, and with the help of an assistant or nurse, doctors can examine and diagnose patients' illnesses.

(Readers will recall, from the first part of this book,
that when James K. Polk came into Tennessee from North
Carolina with his parents, he was a frail, sickly child.
When he was about fourteen, and suffering severely from
an unknown problem, his father took him by horseback
to visit a pioneering young surgeon over in Kentucky. The
doctor diagnosed gallstones and performed surgery, with

only brandy as an anesthesia. In 1839 young Polk would become Tennessee's eleventh governor.)

Now, in 1999, Sundquist, the state's forty-seventh governor, has launched a Southern-wide Task Force on Medical Technology. Under his leadership, this Task Force is looking for ways to expand telemedicine, especially in rural areas, so that no one in the South goes without health care.

Now Governor Sundquist talks to Tennesseans about operations that could occur from miles away, explaining that arthroscopic surgery can be done by looking through a microscope and a computer. "Where this will really help," he explains, "is in rural areas, because health care for rural areas is under siege. Hospitals in these areas are not making it, and in some cases the facilities don't have a sufficient number of patients to allow doctors to keep their skills at expert levels."

Sundquist believes it is important for the South to lead the nation in the use of technology and apply that technology into new areas, areas such as medicine.

Already proud of his state's record of being the first state to place Internet access in every school and library, the present governor sees health care as a state priority. "In Tennessee, our TennCare system is a waiver from Medicaid. There's nothing like it in the country. We've insured every single child in the state, either we've insured them or they have private coverage. No child goes without health care insurance in Tennessee."

As governor, Sundquist's environmental record captured headlines in 1998 when reports showed Tennessee's air, land, and water the cleanest they had been in twenty-five years. He has made the state's pristine beauty one of his priorities, adding seventeen new state natural areas since taking office.

Governor Sundquist has taken numerous state programs and run with them. Without raising taxes, he has initiated unprecedented reforms in the areas of welfare, crime, and government, while placing special emphasis on Tennessee children. His administration's goals for children have been a safe, healthy start; excellence in education; economic opportunity; public safety, and a clean environment.

Sundquist has worked on a bipartisan basis with the Tennessee General Assembly to win approval for programs that further the priorities he has set. In 1996, he won overwhelming bipartisan approval from the General Assembly for Families First, a statewide welfare program designed to move Tennesseans from welfare to work in eighteen months, offering them job training, assistance with transportation, and day care needs.

Since September of that year, the state has seen a 60 percent reduction in the number of employable adults on welfare. Along with this step, he reformed the way the state cares for its needy children by consolidating all services under one department, eliminating duplications of services and taxpayer's money, and more importantly providing better care for both needy and troubled children.

In 1998, the governor hosted the first-ever Governor's Summit on Tennessee's Children, this to bring together families, businesses, churches, schools, and volunteers to offer a brighter future for the children. His TNKids initiative, an outcome of the summit, stresses early intervention and prevention services, as well as coordination of services for families and children at both state and local levels.

In education, Sundquist completed a six-year, $1 billion increase in state funding to Tennessee schools through the Basic Education Program. Through his ConnectTen project, his state became the first one in the nation to connect every public school and library to the Internet. To protect school children from the pornographic material on the net, his state was also the first state to implement software filtering technology on school computers.

In health care, aside from free health insurance to every child who otherwise has no access to coverage, the application of the state's child immunization program is reportedly at an all-time high, while rates of teen pregnancy and infant mortality are at record lows.

On crime, the governor has again worked with the General Assembly to win approval for crime packages that bear down on violent offenders, drunk drivers, and juvenile delinquents. But in spite of his remarkable record, he says serving as the state's governor is his last political office, adding that he doesn't want to be in the Senate, he's been in Congress, he doesn't want to be in anyone's cabinet, and he doesn't want to be an ambassador. He adds that when you've had the best job, you don't want any others.

Sundquist appointed a most diverse cabinet, naming a record number of women to senior posts, as well as naming a number of female judges, so then he must have no qualms at his wife's numerous activities in women's health issues, at-risk children, and education. In 1996, she joined the organizing committee of America Walks for Strong Women, a national event benefiting the National Osteoporosis Foundation. She is also actively involved in raising breast cancer awareness.

As first lady, she serves as an honorary member of the National Advisory Council for Andrew Jackson's The Hermitage, the University of Tennessee's College of Human Ecology, and the Tennessee Federation of Garden Clubs.

Aside from her interests in church and civic organizations, preserving and enhancing Tennessee's beauty is important to Martha Swanson Sundquist, thus she not only works with the state's Federation of Garden Clubs, but also with the Tennessee Department of Transportation, which showcases a variety of beautiful flowers along the state's highways and gateways.

Perhaps she also feels that she's helping emphasize the catchy jingle now applied to the state—"Tennessee

A Reflection

. . . Thus a look into the past, a glimpse so fleeting that it has barely touched upon the valiant deeds of the leaders who have guided the state of Tennessee from the era of the law-of-survival in its wilderness stage to its present period of overflow with the offspring of those inhabitants who were enticed to the area of cheap land and unlimited opportunities. Since that first governorship of the wilderness, the state has moved from an agrarian stage to that of urbanization and then to the retreat-to-the-land again, when those who can afford it look for a spot of Tennessee soil to call their own, away from the traffic and noise of the cities. Those inner cities that were established by the early fathers have become inadequate for business and consumer affairs. Banks and department stores and shops and supermarkets huddle in the suburbs, away from the cobblestone streets so painstakingly laid by the descendents of those emigrants who pushed out from England and France, detouring for a period to North Carolina and Virginia as they got together households and families, their descendents to push on into the new state of Tennessee which would bear their marks in its structures and their names in its legends and statutes.

By the latter part of the 1970s, Tennesseans had paused to reflect on the state's glorious past, and had brought many of its heroes into historical perpetuity. Andrew Jackson and John Sevier had been immortalized in stone in the nation's hall of fame in Washington, and the statue of Sevier's first wife. Sara Hawkins Sevier, was unveiled to a smaller group on Knoxville's courthouse lawn. Andrew Johnson's tailor shop, once merely the working place of a common tailor, was reevaluated and labeled as an honorable state marker in Greeneville where his tomb became a national marker. The Hermitage, Andrew Jackson's estate in Nashville, had long since become a notable historical site, along with the James Polk home in Columbia. There followed a period when numerous residences of the state's giants were looked at anew and restored for preservation.

Rocky Mount, the site of Tennessee's first state capital, had been acquired by the state and filed to historical antiquity. State parks across the state opened up, proudly wearing the names of governors and national leaders, with the David Crockett State Park in Lawrence County marking the nineteenth such establishment. But some of the memorials bore a more dignified repose than the leisure-ridden fascade of parks, such as the resting place of Governor Roane in Knox County (Pleasant Forest Cemetery), which was designated a state burial ground in 1939; or more scholarly characteristics, such as the Austin Peay State College in Clarksville.

The state capitol had been repaired and renovated, and the governor's mansion, frowned upon by frugal nineteenth-century Tennesseans, had become a place of esteem in the mind of pompous twentieth-centurians. Consequently, in 1949, the state purchased the Georgian residence "Farhills" (built originally for William Ridley Wills) with an accompanying ten acres of land on Curtiswood Lane in

Nashville, which has become the new governor's mansion, and remains the lovely home of the state's first families.

Tennesseans had their own state flower (iris) and their state bird (mockingbird), and in 1947 the legislature designated the tulip poplar as the state tree. They had their own flag too, where boldly, against a red background, three white stars represented the three grand divisions of the state—East, Middle, and West Tennessee.

Governor Dunn, emphasizing unity within the state, struck out at the division so long acknowledged by Tennesseans, but it still remains. Lee S. Greene, writing in *Government in Tennessee*, even maintains such diversity is good, for it creates distinctiveness and revives the past, and possibly political variety as "particular areas of the country have held to particular politics." Greene continued, "The differences were brought on primarily by the conflicts of Civil War and Reconstruction, and the patterns of politics set then continued to be reflected in the allotment of voters between the Republican and Democratic parties until the 1970s. East Tennessee became and remained Republican, Middle and West Tennessee, with substantial numbers of Whigs, became and remained Democratic (because the Republicans were associated with a bitter reconstruction period)." [1]

This publication, because it has dealt with the winners and not the losers, has been concerned with the major political movements only; but Tennessee has known something of the Independents, too—Populists (1892), Progressives (1912 and 1924), Dixiecrats (1948), and the American party (1968).

Throughout all its hassles, the province has proudly hailed itself the Volunteer State, and abiding by the ethos

[1]Lee S. Greene, David H. Grubbs, Victor C. Hobday, *Government in Tennessee* (Knoxville: University of Tennessee Press, 3rd ed., 1975), 62.

of its past, responded to the Asian wars of the '50s and '60s, sending over 10,000 men to the Korean conflict and thousands more to the Vietnam War. In 1967, when resentment flared against the government for involvement in a war that many felt need not concern the United States, and when not-so-patriotic Americans were snatching the Stars and Stripes from places of honor, hurling the hallowed fabric under their feet in heated moments of anger, or setting it with flames in a more heated fury, Tennessee lawmakers—with traditional zeal—adopted a measure favoring the government's policy in Vietnam, and passed a law to provide stringent punishment for the desecration of the United States flag.

The state seal, first created under Governor Roane and altered slightly under Governor Brownlow, labeled the state from the start a procurer of agriculture. So it has remained through the years, not only picturesque with its rolling pastures in the Tennessee walking horse country, but also ranking high in production of farm products. In spite of the present high economy that has necessitated the transfer of farm-to-industry employment, agriculture continues to be a major business in Tennessee. The 1976 farm census showed 124,000 farms still in operation in the state; and with the new developments in commercial fertilizers and fungicides, production per acre is at an all-time high as those who farm the land turn to more efficient farm operations.

Like its sister states, the Volunteer State has come from the period of the pioneer to the apparent final frontier of the space age. But to modern man who may visit city after city within Tennessee's boundaries with relative ease and speed—whether he travels by car and the "freeways" or by air in this awesome day of discoveries—the thoughts of earlier Tennesseans struggling over hills and down valleys to their destinations that took days enroute seem like fairy tales.

Yet, there remains the determination of the state's historical thought-leaders to keep alive for those who come after them the memoirs of earlier statesmen, and this book has borne a few of them. Possibly the records of the past will help to fortify future leaders of the state as they grapple with more people and more problems on limited land; where they must learn to work out their problems together on one earth, for there is no other . . . .

Roster of Governors

STATE OF FRANKLIN

John Sevier	1784

TERRITORY SOUTH OF THE RIVER OHIO

William Blount	1790-1796

·STATE OF TENNESSEE

`John Sevier	1796-1801; 1803-1809
Archibald Roane	1801-1803
Willie Blount	1809-1815
Joseph McMinn	1815-1821
William Carroll	1821-1827; 1829-1835
Sam Houston	1827-April, 1829
William Hall	April, 1829-October, 1829
Newton Cannon	1835-1839
James Knox Polk	1839-1841
James Chamberlain Jones	1841-1845
Aaron Vail Brown	1845-1847

Neill S. Brown	1847-1849
William Trousdale	1849-1851
William Bowen Campbell	1851-1853
Andrew Johnson	1853-1857; 1862-1865
(military governor)	
Isham Green Harris	1857-1862
Robert Looney Caruthers (never inaugurated)	1863
William Gannaway Brownlow	1865-1869
DeWitt Clinton Senter	1869-1871
John Calvin Brown	1871-1875
James Davis Porter	1875 1879
Albert Smith Marks	1879-1881
Alvin Hawkins	1881-1883
William Brimage Bate	1883-1887
Robert Love Taylor	1887-1891; 1897-1899
John Price Buchanan	1891-1893
Peter Turney	1893-1897
Benton McMillin	1899-1903
James Beriah Frazier	1903-1905
John Isaac Cox	1905-1907
Malcolm R. Patterson	1907-1911
Ben Walter Hooper	1911-1915
Thomas C. Rye	1915-1919
Albert H. Roberts	1919-1921
Alfred A. Taylor	1921-1923
Austin Peay	1923-1927
Henry H. Horton	1927-1933
Hill McAlister	1933-1937
Gordon Browning	1937-1939; 1949-1953
Prentice Cooper	1939-1945
Jim Nance McCord	1945-1949
Frank Goad Clement	1953-1959; 1963-1967
Buford Ellington	1959-1963; 1967-1971
Winfield C. Dunn	1971-1975
Ray Blanton	1975-

Bibliography

BOOKS

Allison, John (ed.). *Notable Men of Tennessee,* Vol. 2. Atlanta: Southern Historical Association, 1905.

de Camp, L. Sprague. *The Great Monkey Trial.* Garden City: Doubleday and Company, 1968.

Caldwell, Joshua W. *Sketches of the Bench and Bar.* Knoxville: Ogden Brothers and Company, 1898.

Caldwell, Mary French. *Tennessee, The Volunteer State* Chicago: Richtext press, 1968.

Clayton, W.W. *Davidson County Tennesse* (reprint of 1880 edition). Nashville: Charles Elder, 1971.

Driver, Carl S. *John Sevier, Pioneer of the Old Southwest.* Nashville: Charles and Randy Booksellers, 1973

Dykemean, Wilma, *Tennesse: A Bicentennial History.* New York: W.W. Norton and Company, 1975.

Folmsbee, Stanley J.; Corlew, Robert E.; Mitchell, Enoch L. *Tennessee: A Short History.* Knoxville: A University of Tennessee Press, 1972.

Gerson, Noel B. *The Yankee from Tennessee.* Garden City: Doubleday and Company, 1960.

Green, John W. *Lives of the Judges of the Supreme Court of Tennessee.* Knoxville: Archer and Smith, 1947.

Green, Lee S.; Grubbs, David H.; Hobday, Victor C. *Government in Tennessee.* Knoxville: University of Tennessee Press, 1975.

Hammer, Phillips M. *Tennessee: A History,* Vol. 6. New York: American Historical Society, 1933.

Masterson, William H. *William Blount* (Second Edition). New York: Greenwood Press, 1969.

McGee, Gentry R. *A History of Tennessee* (facsimile reproduction of 1927 edition). Nashville: Charles Elder, 1971.

McKallar, Kenneth. *Tennessee Senators.* Kingsport, Tenn.: Southern Publishers, Inc., 1942.

Merrit, Dixon L. *History of Tennessee and Tennesseans,* Vol. 4. Chicago: Lewis Publishing Company, 1913.

Moore, John Trotwood. *The Volunteer State,* Vol. 6. Chicago: S.J. Clarke Publishing Company, 1923.

Moritz, Charles. *Current Biography Yearbook,* The H.B. Wilson Company, New York, 1991

Morrel, Martha M. *Young Hickory, The Life and Times of President James K. Polk.* New York: Ives Washburn, Inc., 1965

Scopes, John T., and Presley, James. *Center of the Storm Memoirs of John T. Scopes.* New York: Holt, Rinehart, and Winston, 1967.

Severn, Bill. *Frontier President: The Life of James K. Polk.* New York: Ives Washburn, Inc., 1967.

Severn, Bill In Lincoln's Footsteps: The Life of Andrew Johnson. New York: Ives Washburn, Inc, 1966.

Speer, William S. (ed.). *Prominent Tennesseans.* Nashville: Albert B Travel, 1888.

Stewart, John Craig. *The Governors of Alabama* Gretna, La.: Pelican Publishing Company, 1975.

Walker, Nancy Wooten. *Out of a Clear Blue Sky: Lives of Tennessee First Ladies* Knoxville: Nancy Walker, 1971.

White, Robert H. *Messages of the Governors,* Vol. 1. Nashville: Tennessee Historical Commission, 1952.

——. *Messages of the Governors,* Vol. 5. Nashville: Tennessee Historical Commission, 1959.

——. *Messages of the Governors of Alabama.* Vol. 6. Nashville: Tennessee Historical Commission, 1963.

White, Robert H. *Tennessee: Its Growth and Progress.* Nashville: Robert White, 1947.

Williams, Samuel Cole. *History of the State of Franklin.* Johnson City, Tenn.: Watauga Press, 1924.

OTHER PUBLICATIONS

Biographical Directory of the American Congress.

Blanton, Ray. Governor's Mansion, Written Interview.

William Brownlow Papers, Manusript Section, Tennessee State Library.

Castel, Albert. "Andrew Jackson-A Profile," A Profile," *American History Illustrated,* (October, 1969), p. 4.

Dunn, Winfield, Hospital Corporation of America, Nashville: Written Interview.

Federal Writer's Project, Manuscript Section, Tennessee State Library.

Journal of Muscle Shoals History, Vol. 10 (Tennessee Valley Historical Society; 1983), 114, and Vol. 11 (Tennessee Valley Historical Society: 1986), 21

Nashville Banner

Nashville Tennessean, Jan. 18, 1987; Nov. 23, 1996; Nov. 25, 1996; and Nov. 14, 1997, clippings from Tennessee State Library files.

Thomas Clarke Rye Papers, Manuscript Section, Tennessee State Library.

Tennessee Blue Book. Nashville: (1954, 1967, 1968, 1975, 1976, 1979, 1987, 1988, 1995, 1996 editions.)

Tennessee Historical Society, Biographical Sketches, Tennessee State Library.

Unpublished McWherter biographies, prepared by Mrs. Lucille McWherter, Tennessee State Library Files

William Trousdale Papers, Manuscript Section, Tennessee State Library.

William Ridley Wills Papers, Manuscript Section, Tennessee State Library.

Index